Outside
the Box

Cardboard Design Now

black dog
publishing
london uk

Contents

Foreword

A material considered as predominantly practical, cardboard's increasing use in art and design suggests it is a material of endless possibilities that dismisses the staid and uninspiring reputation with which it has become associated. Its malleability, surprising durability—particularly when combined with other materials—recyclability, and sustainability, all contribute to cardboard's growing appeal within today's creative industries.

From its original association with the humble cardboard box, cardboard's use within packaging design has evolved to include myriad designs—from the wholly practical, to more complicated concepts with numerous functions that, on occasions, blur the line between packaging and product. Recently adopted by product designers, cardboard is viewed as a thrifty material with which to work, proving popular in the production of items as varied as children's toys, lighting and stereo speakers. In comparison, its some-what lengthy history with furniture design, due to its experimental appeal and association with sustainable design, continue to drive its use—proving its often doubted strength and durability to be mistaken, with tables, chairs and even beds being included within the following pages. Lastly, cardboard's presence within art and architecture must not go unnoticed—here shown together in a nod to the plethora of cardboard installations considered to be both art and architecture; promoting the material's possibilities in large-scale, as whole structures built from cardboard are depicted.

Documenting both the practical and the fantastical, *Outside the Box: Cardboard Design Now* is a comprehensive look at this versatile material, showing how it is used in a creative, artistic and, of course, functional way, whilst simultaneously, suggesting the medium as open to further possibilities.

opposite
Cardboard Café (detail)
2009.
Courtesy B3 Designers.

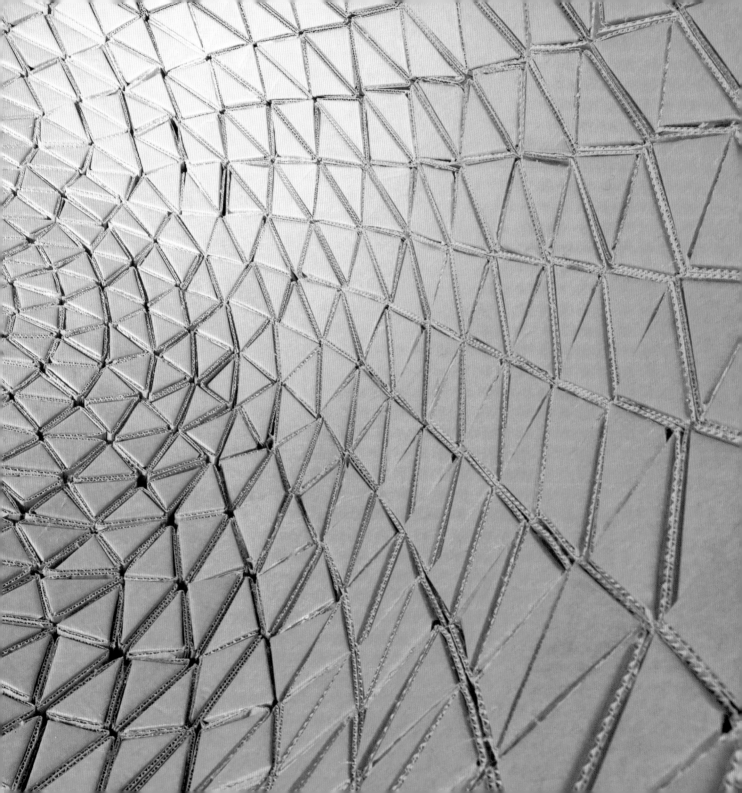

The Cardboard Story Unfolds

Michael Czerwinski

For much of its life cardboard has been perceived as paper's poor relation, far removed from the much revered hybrid parent material. Though initially designed with durability and disposability in mind, cardboard has risen from the anonymity of a utilitarian product; it is almost fair to say that it is now imbued with a desirability to rival any creative material. This change of purpose has not been sudden and is not conclusive, but the recent proliferation of its use in design and art is asserting cardboard as a legitimate creative material.

As a product, paper has an almost infinite amount of creative and industrial uses. It has an ancient history spanning millennia, starting as a prized and rare commodity and ending up today as a schizophrenic material that is either opulently watermarked or anonymously throwaway. Cardboard has made a very different journey.

Its recent roots lie in the functionality of a secondary product conceived as a packaging material to protect more valued primary objects; to serve rather than to lead. It is now undergoing a transformation of perception not only by artists and designers but also consumers. We are witnessing the maturing of a comparatively young material which is now being celebrated, rather than shunned, for its own unique qualities

The world seems ready to accept the potential of cardboard. All our lives we have been exposed to corrugated variants of cardboard, scored and folded into boxes and packaging inserts. This familiarity seems to have acted as a smoke screen, blinding us to the potential of the material. Today, however, this has changed somewhat—thanks to a generation or so of creative pioneers.

To understand current attitudes towards cardboard it is necessary to reflect on how perception of the material has evolved. The cardboard box has become a ubiquitous genre of product that we accept with the same unguarded attitude as we project onto the wheel or the chair. It is there because it works, and works so well that it requires forced motivation to challenge its validity. It is hard to imagine a time before cardboard existed as its very invention has influenced the systems that validate how products can be manufactured and then distributed to create the choice and satisfy the demand in our consumerist world. Current ecology and sustainability concerns will change how the box is made, shaped, used and reused but it will never be discarded altogether. The fact is that the cardboard box has always come in an infinite variety of conjugations, and its design and application will continue to evolve as required.

However, it is testament to the inherent qualities of cardboard that allow us to look upon the box as a genre. We see the thinness of the material in relationship to the scale of the structure and the embossed crease that allows the box to open. We feel the rhythmically ribbed corrugation

opposite
Honeycomb (series detail)
2010.
Courtesy Lazerian
and Richard Sweeney.

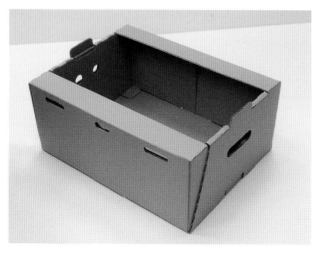

through the surface layer of board and are reassured by the rigid strength in relation to its light weight. We smell the dulled aromas of wood fibre and adhesive romantically associated with countless memories of receiving new packages. We can all conjure up in our minds a generic pictogram of a cardboard box as universal as the symbols that communicate light bulb or lightning. But unlike the generic chair, for example, the history of cardboard and its most closely associated product are recent enough inventions to still be able to track.

Corrugated papers have been around for centuries, with examples apparent as far back as fifteenth century China. More recently, there is reference to the first commercially manufactured cardboard box produced in the United Kingdom in 1817, though this would have probably been made of a thin solid board. The invention of the first corrugated cardboard box is attributed to the American Robert Gair in 1890. However, cardboard as we know it today was gradually evolved prior to this over the course of the second half of the nineteenth century with a corrugated board first patented in 1856 in the United Kingdom. This flexible low cost material was used as a liner to support the drums of gentlemen's top hats. Its life continued beyond the manufacture of this ephemeral fashion item when a patent was requested in 1871 by New York based Albert Jones for a product that consisted of a corrugation lined on

one side with a single sheet of flat board. This was used to wrap around bottles and other cylindrical glass products as protective packaging. The design was further improved in 1874 by Oliver Long who sought a patent for the now familiar product lined on both sides with a flat board.

In true urban myth style, New York based paper bag printer Robert Gair was careless one day with a metal ruler whilst plying his trade and cut through a stack of paper with the sharp metal edge. This led him to devise a technique of mechanically cutting and scoring corrugated cardboard using a punching method and by 1895 the first fully formed pre-cut ready-to-fold cardboard boxes were in full production. Cheaper, thinner, and lighter to produce than a wooden crate, the cardboard box was quickly adopted by manufactures of all types of goods as a way to provide protection during transit for vulnerable items.

The impact this would have on manufacturing would be highly significant. As the Industrial Revolution thrust its way through the nineteenth century it was establishing the foundations for what we now refer to as a global economy. Manufacturing was no longer only satisfying local demand but potentially catering to nationwide and international markets. A growing prosperity also created a middle class with an increasing disposable income. The Steam Age made it possible to transport goods quickly and cheaply across vast distances by rail and sea. People expected to have access to

left
Cardboard Crate
Peter Skinner.
Courtesy the artist.

right
Mr Popple's Chocolate packaging
100 per cent recycled cardboard, printed using rubber stamps and water based inks. Designed by KO Creative.

their familiar commodities wherever they might be in the world. This combination of circumstance, opportunity and desire fuelled the need to be able to transport all manner of merchandise. Technology was being used to create and satisfy the needs of a society changing at an unprecedented rate, and the humble cardboard box had its part to play in streamlining the manufacturing and transportation process. Cheap, strong and lightweight, it was an anonymous object that could transgress society, culture, and class.

The cardboard box is also a vehicle for branding and can be a core element within the design and establishment of a product. The Kellogg's Company was one of the first food producers to use cartons as a way of packaging cereal. Initially, the corn flakes went directly into the box, which was then wrapped in an airtight bag. When this system was inverted the opportunity was created to use the surfaces of the carton to advertise the product as well as the manufacturer. This was then supported by constant brand reinforcement every time the breakfast bowl was filled or kitchen cupboard opened.

The cereal carton has been a constant resource for home craft activities for many a creative child. It is a waste product with happy associations that feel substantial and complete, but ok to deface and manipulate. This is a rare combination of emotive high regard, and freedom to destroy, to make something new and personal. Cardboard is treated as a playful material because it is so readily available and mostly unvalued. This is greatly liberating for the creative process where the artist can be lifted from the burdens of expensive materials, technical processes and prescribed results. If it doesn't matter if the thing being made goes wrong, the creative endeavour is more likely to be uninhibited. There is truth in the cliché that kids spend more time playing with the boxes their toys arrive in, as this part of the product experience allows them to manifest any creative thought without reprimand, rules or lasting repercussions.

No other craft material allows for the instant gratification of constructing reasonably large structures at low cost and low effort. It is no wonder that cardboard is the material of choice for many designers and architects working through design problems by making three-dimensional sketches. Acclaimed Italian designer Mario Bellini still works in this way in spite of the array of available modelling software and his extensive personal experience.

The ironic design gesture is an appropriation of the material that has haunted cardboard over recent years. How thought provoking it is to see packaging out of context! The Boiler House project at the Victoria and Albert Museum in the 1980s set about to pioneer the appreciation of twentieth century product and industrial design within a gallery context. At the time this was a radical move, especially at an institution renowned for its historic applied arts collections.

left
Cardboard ring box
Cardboard and paint.
Courtesy Sruli Recht and Snorri Már Snorrason.

right
Mod Lambretta
Chris Gilmore.
2004.
Cardboard and glue.
Courtesy the artist, Perugi Artecontemporanea.
Photo Marco De Palma.

In the initial displays the exhibits were placed on plinths that were blatantly cardboard boxes. This was a combination of supposedly ordinary everyday household objects sitting on the most ordinary of items to reinforce that this was, conceptually, a different type of exhibition. In hindsight this helped legitimise cardboard as a material appropriate for furniture and interiors. Less than ten years later the Crafts Council was using white cardboard structures to display the work of British applied artists at international trade shows in the US. This was no longer an ironic statement but a practical solution to producing a uniform display that could flat pack for easy transit. Today whole interiors—such as offices for the Dutch PR agency Nothing, designed by Arik Koudenburg and Joost van Bleiswijk—are being built out of cardboard. This architectural structure alludes to the loadbearing strength and permanence of a Rolled Steel Joist aesthetic with pared down detail and simplification of form. The tension between implied permanence and rational awareness of transience is further teased by office workers' marker pen doodles on the walls. This is an environment that cleverly infers a nurturing of creative and independent thinking amongst the team that work within it, as well as about the agency, which this approach helps to brand.

Today, cardboard is on the brink of being used without the constraints of having to apologetically refer to its humble beginnings. Laser cutting technology allows it to be rendered with accuracy and precision. Three-dimensional modelling computer programmes make possible complicated cut and fold mapping to create flat pack patterns to be folded and glued into faceted structures. Digital printing is used to apply colour, image and text onto surfaces at low cost. Most importantly the intention and spirit is there amongst new generations of artists and designers to choose this material because of its qualities and potential.

Frank Gehry's early 1970s Easy Edges collection is an obvious example of the pursuit of form influenced by the structural engineering potential of cardboard. These layered forms work on the principle that alternating the direction of the corrugation between layers of cardboard, within a block of laminated sheets, creates a remarkably sturdy structure. This is demonstrated to flamboyant extent in the curvaceously counter lever eluding Side Chair, 1972. This is a worthy example of the tradition of architect conceived iconic chair design that embodies the spirit of the time, and conviction of its creator. In recent years this flat facet laminate style has been an appropriate vehicle for tapping into the trend of extravagantly retro pop styled interiors. The chunky and geometrically clean lined shelves designed by Reinhard Dienes fit perfectly into any discerning stripped backed, white-washed pad to work both as a dramatic conversation piece as well as somewhere to display carefully selected designer objects.

left
Nothing office interior
2009.
Courtesy Nothing
and Joost Van Bleiswijk.

centre
Side Chair
1971.
61 x 35 x 87 cm.
Frank Gehry.
Copyright Vitra,
www.vitra.com.

right
Bravais Armchair
Computer-modelled image
2010.
Courtesy Lazerian
and Richard Sweeney.

The eclectic collection of furniture and accessories designed by London based Giles Miller embodies the current spirit of content-led cross-disciplinary design. These are not cardboard objects but objects that happen to be made out of cardboard. They show the potential of the material but still have the presence and personality to exist in their own right.

Cardboard is used with a sense of neutrality in the epic computer plotted faceted structure depicting an Everest inspired mountainous landscape by artist George Morris in his installation *Hall of Mountains* 2009. This site-specific sculpture is meant to evoke a sense of inhospitable place depicted in an ephemeral material that allows the viewer to voyeuristically experience it as if looking at a three-dimensional photograph.

The future will bring further potential and challenges for cardboard. New technologies will give designers opportunities to experiment and push creative endeavour. The material will continue to evolve as a discipline and genre. It will be play an increasingly prevalent role in our designed surroundings, and boxes will always be needed to put things in. Sustainability issues will also play a part in this process. Puma's 2010 launch at the Design Museum of Yves Behar's Clever Little Bag demonstrates that there is strong collateral in challenging the eco credentials of packaging. The cardboard box is no longer anonymous or to be disregarded or discarded. It has become a weapon with which manufacturers can demonstrate sustainability awareness by cleverly reducing the weight, volume and longevity of what their products are wrapped in. Cardboard is now fully empowered and primed as a creative medium, design solution or eco warrior.

left
Georgia Sideboard
(detail)
2010.
Corrugated cardboard.
60 x 120 cm.
Courtesy Reinhard Dienes.

right top
Pool Rocker II
2009.
Corrugated cardboard.
56 x 67 x 78 cm.
Courtesy Giles Miller.

right bottom
Clever Little Bag
Yves Behar.
2010.
Courtesy Puma.

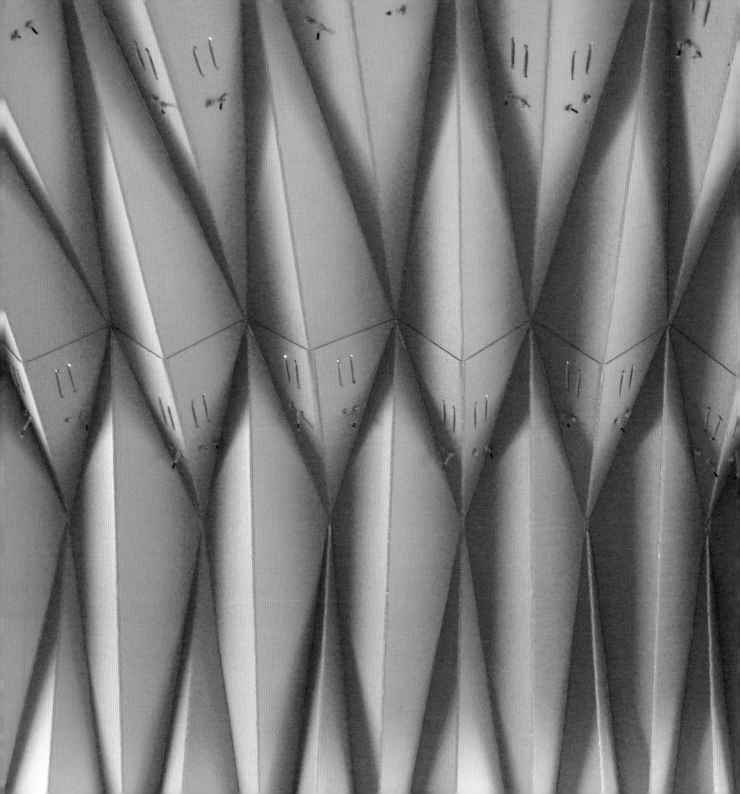

Cardboard— Structural and Material Innovation

Santiago R Perez

Cardboard is a relatively modern material, developed in China as early as the second century AD. Kraft paper, the raw material used in the production of cardboard, is made from the pulp of fast-growing pine trees, using a process developed by Swedish chemist Carl F Dahl in 1884. The main characteristic of cardboard, in comparison with paper, is its weight: "Paper with a weight class above 250 gram/m^2 is known as cardboard."[1] From this Kraft paper based raw material, several types of cardboard products used primarily in the packaging industry have recently been adopted for research and development of cardboard architecture: corrugated cardboard, honeycomb core panels, and paper tube cylindrical structural members.

Corrugated cardboard, the ubiquitous pleated Kraft paper packaging material, was patented in 1856 by two English inventors, Healey & Allen, and later developed into the cardboard box that we see everywhere today, by an American named Robert Gair, in 1871. The most interesting and useful aspect of the manufacturing process is the almost unlimited, endless roll production process, in mechanised production plants 90 metres in length, or more. These automated machines combine a minimum of two face liners with the internal flutes or corrugated layer, using cornstarch glue. The process of heating, gluing and pressing the Kraft paper results in a continuous stream of corrugated paper that is cut into blanks and formed into boxes.

Honeycomb Core

Structural sandwich panels utilise a variety of hexagonal core materials and were first developed by Norman de Bruyne, a physicist and aeronautical materials scientist specialising in adhesives and composite materials. The most famous use of early honeycomb core panels was in the construction of the de Havilland Mosquito Bomber, utilising wood sandwich construction with a balsa core. The noted American architect Craig Ellwood began using lightweight honeycomb structural sandwich panels in the 1950s, as epitomised in his Californian Case Study House No. 18. Ellwood's architecture, and sandwich panel construction in general, were emblematic of California's climate responsive, modern, lightweight 'machine architecture' as opposed to earlier craft-based construction.

Paper honeycomb core panels were being tested and researched as a construction material as early as 1956, by the US Forest Products Laboratory. Sandwich panels are composed of core construction with the cellular pattern perpendicular to the outer facing layers. The most crucial aspect of production is the continuity of the bond between the core material and facings, and the use of resin-impregnated, water-resistant cores, made possible by modern adhesives and chemicals that

opposite
Cardboard Banquet (detail) 2008.
Corrugated cardboard.
Courtesy Cambridge University Department of Architecture.

have evolved over time to include formaldehyde-free, fully recycled and recyclable core and facing materials. Today, honeycomb panels are used in the packaging industry, in automotive products, and as lightweight door panels and interior partitions. The renewed interest in honeycomb core panels has given rise to new architectural applications, such as the interior office walls designed by Ro&AdArchitecten in Eindhoven in 2005.

Paper-Tube

By far the most utilised form of Kraft paper product in architectural applications is the spiral wound cardboard tube: "Paper tubes, the form of paper most associated with [Shigeru] Ban, actually begin with rolls of recycled paper. These are cut into strips, saturated with glue, and wound spirally around a short metal rod that creates the hollow core of the tube." The compressive strength of cardboard tube is about half that of similarly sized wood or bamboo structural members. The fully recyclable nature of this material, combined with its extreme lightness or strength to weight ratio, provides compelling reasons for use in architectural applications including temporary shelters, exhibition pavilions and experimental structures. The ease of manufacturing paper tubes in any length, diameter or thickness has

proved to be one of the primary advantages of this material in developing paper tube structures for architecture. The pioneering use of paper tubes by architect Shigeru Ban has led him to describe paper as "evolved wood". "Paper tubes, the form of paper most associated with Ban, actually begin with rolls of recycled paper. These are cut into strips, saturated with glue, and wound spirally around a short metal rod that creates the hollow core of the tube."[2]

Future Form:
Towards an Eco-Material Economy

Cardboard may be considered the ultimate "cradle-to-cradle" material for architecture, due to its ability to transform an everyday industrial product into the raw material for an ecologically sustainable future. The low embodied energy of paper-based materials, combined with post-consumer waste-stream repurposing or recycling of paper and cardboard products into raw construction material, represents a relatively huge, untapped potential for development of new architectural materials and systems.

The increasing desire for ecologically sustainable architecture has created a renewed interest in emerging practices based on the evolving aesthetics of 'lightness' characteristic of both twentieth and twenty-first century modernism. Paper-based cardboard architecture, pioneered

left
Beast office
2008.
Honeycomb cardboard.
Courtesy Paul Coudamy.

right
Vasareley Pavillion (detail)
Aix-en-Provence, France,
2006.
Paper tubes.
Courtesy Shigeru
Ban Architects.

primarily by Shigeru Ban, has a unique position within emerging practices. The extreme lightness and low cost of corrugated cardboard sheets, honeycomb panels, and paper tube structures, creates unprecedented opportunities for paper-based design, still largely in its infancy. Of the three categories mentioned, by far the most tested and well documented system is based on paper tube components, combined with overlapping or axial connectors and bracing, to create large-scale, lightweight spanning structures, as exemplified by Ban's 22 metre-high *Paper Tower*, built for the London Design Festival, 2009.

Structures made from the direct stacking of corrugated sheets or recycled "bales" constitute another category of experimental cardboard architecture. Post-consumer cardboard was used directly as a recycled raw construction material in the 2001 Rural Studio project in Newbern, Alabama. While the recycling of cardboard is made difficult due to the wax-impregnated coating used to protect the material from moisture, the Newbern project brought attention to the potential of cardboard as a relatively obscure architectural material. The acoustic listening environment *Mafoombey*, designed by Finnish architecture students Kalliala and Ruskeepää, was fabricated using 720 layers of uniquely shaped individual sheets of corrugated cardboard.

The primary challenges facing the designer in developing cardboard architecture include fire safety, protection from rain and humidity, and the structural characteristics of each type of material system, from the relative weakness of corrugated sheets, to the de-lamination or 'creep' associated with paper tube systems. These challenges are, paradoxically, part of cardboard's inherent attractiveness as an experimental material, as they stem from the primary advantages of using a cellulose-based, easily demountable and recyclable material—cardboard's extreme lightness and economy of means.

Surface Architecture:
Corrugated and Honeycomb Structures

Recent interest in alternative materials and practices in architecture have produced a developing culture of experimentation, combining both the advances in digitally generated complex geometries, with a return to simple materials and forms inspired by nature. Architects are increasingly interested in the mathematical, geometric and engineering principles underlying natural forms, moving beyond aesthetics, to discover the structural efficiency of nature.

One of the most easily observed aspects of this renewed interest in nature is the complex patterning of surfaces and

left
Paper Tower
London Design Festival, 2009.
Paper tubes.
Courtesy Shigeru
Ban Architects.
Photo Susan Smart
Photography.

right
Mafoombey
2005.
Corrugated cardboard.
250 x 250 x 250 cm.
Courtesy Kalliala,
Ruskeepaa and Lukasczyk.

forms in recent architecture, borrowing ideas from origami, mathematical concepts and biologically inspired materials.

Contemporary architecture increasingly reflects a desire for economy of material, and efficiency in structure and form, often combined with a concern for the ecological and social potential of design. These tendencies have produced a renewed interest in material exploration, digital fabrication and expanded practice, as illustrated in the Liechtenstein University of Applied Sciences model-making annex, fabricated entirely out of interlocking cardboard components. This emerging architecture requires a re-thinking of material practice, borrowing concepts from the automotive, aerospace and product design disciplines, as Kieran and Timberlake demonstrated in their manifesto "Refabricating Architecture". Within this context, cardboard surface architecture may be classified as either corrugated folded surfaces, or honeycomb gridcore panel systems.

The application of origami concepts to architecture poses several challenges. The rapidly emerging field of contemporary paper origami, while rooted in the well known animal shapes typical of traditional Japanese folded paper constructions, now employs sophisticated mathematical modeling techniques, resulting in myriad new generations of folded or pleated geometries, as seen in the work of Richard Sweeney. Folded surfaces

have been explored in architecture primarily utilising concrete as a building material, as in the Pallazodello Sport—the 1960 Olympic Stadium in Rome, designed by Pier Luigi Nervi.

More recently, architects interested in cardboard as a building material have looked to paper origami for inspiration, primarily for the construction of temporary structures. The *Cardboard Banquet* folded plate temporary installation project, led by paper product designer Rentaro Nishimura, was fabricated as a test of the application of origami concepts using corrugated cardboard in a pleated roof assembly. The highly efficient form of this temporary structure was fabricated by students at Cambridge University from overlapping plates of folded cardboard, fastened with simple rope connections.

The structural efficiency and strength of paper-based materials may be greatly increased through the use of honeycomb panels, especially when utilised in a composite cardboard and plywood system, as pioneered in the roof structure of the Nemunoki Children's Art Museum, by Shigeru Ban, constructed in 1999. This composite panel roof system was fabricated using triangular module assemblies, with each panel made from two layers of paper honeycomb gridcore sandwiched around a plywood core. This open-cell lattice structure allows natural light to enter from above,

left
Surface
Piazza Citadella, Lucca, Italy, 2007.
Cardboard waterproofed with PVA.
400 x 200 x 200 cm.
Courtesy the artist.
Photo Richard Sweeney.

right
Cardboard Banquet
2008.
Corrugated cardboard.
Courtesy Cambridge University Department of Architecture.

achieving stability by means of aluminium plate and pipe connections, resulting in a free spanning space, reducing the number of required supporting columns.

One of the most promising applications of cardboard design in architecture is in the development of easily transportable, prefabricated low-cost emergency or short-term shelters. The prototype Cardboard House by Australian architects Stutchbury and Pape, is a flat-pack kit of parts lightweight dwelling constructed from laminated cardboard panels, structural frames and beams. The prototype was built for the House of the Future exhibition, in association with the University of Sydney in 2005. The interlocking flat-packed frames are conceived as easily assembled systems inspired by the use of cardboard as packaging material.

The use of cardboard in temporary exhibition architecture provides opportunities for experimental material innovation, however the goal of utilising corrugated or honeycomb panels as a permanent construction system requires a much greater investment in research towards fire safety and structural limitations of panels systems. One of the most thoroughly engineered and tested flat-panel cardboard architecture research projects is the Westborough Cardboard Classroom project, developed by BuroHappold engineers and the architecture firm Cottrell and Vermeulen in 2001, in association with Dr Andrew

Cripps. Utilising flat panels as the primary enclosure system in combination with paper tube columns and wood beams, the project exemplifies the potential of incorporating composite material strategies in the development of permanent cardboard architecture.

Alternatives to Kraft paper-based cardboard materials may be the key to future architecture using sustainable, natural construction materials. Research towards more efficient production and greater structural capacity of honeycomb sandwich panels and corrugated cardboard materials is an evolving science. The development of "Ecotextiles" or fibre-based natural raw materials, including kenaf, hemp and jute, are increasingly replacing synthetics in the development of new materials. Within this context, the development of cardboard architecture provides an incentive to industry for replacing synthetic materials with negative environmental impacts, with sustainable natural fibre renewable materials. Natural fibre composites, made from a combination of recycled plastic and fibrous materials, may provide a solution for eliminating the moisture protection issues surrounding cardboard construction, and lead the way towards future architectural construction systems.

left
Cardboard House
2007.
Courtesy Peter Sutchbury Architecture.

right
Westborough Cardboard Classroom
1999.
Composite cardboard. panels and cardboard tubes.
Courtesy Cottrell and Vermeulen Architecture.
Photo Peter Grant Photography.

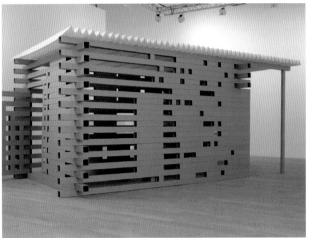

Efficiency and Lightness:
Paper-Tube Structures

Japan has officially recognised paper tube structures as an authorised material for permanent construction since 1993. Structural testing of paper tubes has been a well-documented aspect of pioneering experiments by Ban, in association with Dr Minoru Tezuka at Waseda University in Tokyo.

Paper tube architecture may generally be described as constructed from vertically aligned tubes in compression, and horizontally oriented or curved 'grid shell' structures with more complex geometries. Vertical tube structures must negotiate the vertical structural loads as well as wind and other dynamic lateral forces, caused by earthquakes, for example. The paper tubes are connected with laminated wood or steel connections, and braced by diagonal cables. Ban's first permanent vertical tube structure was the *Library of a Poet*, built in 1991, and was later followed by his *Paper House*, of 1995. The most well known work utilising vertical paper tubes is perhaps Ban's *Paper Church*, built in Japan in 1995 as a response to the Great Hanshin earthquake in Kobe.

The directness and simplicity of form and ease of assembly characteristic of these lightweight structures, evokes references to both traditional, vernacular architecture, such as that utilised by nomadic cultures, and also suggests a new, more enlightened approach to building ecologically and socially responsive structures in the twenty-first century.

Perhaps the most compelling use of paper tube or cardboard architecture capturing the imagination of both the public and emerging architects, is the doubly-curved lattice or 'grid shell' structure. These curved, free-spanning structures may be seen as an evolution of the simple dome or single-span roofs, such as Ban's *Paper Dome* of 1998, built to withstand snow loads from multiple sections of straight tubes. Grid shell structures employ the doubly-curved geometry, and continuous curvature of long paper tube sections, as a sophisticated solution to both free-spans and lateral forces in architecture. The most famous example of this type of architecture is the *Japan Pavilion*, built for the Hanover Expo 2000, and designed by Ban in collaboration with the famous German architect of lightweight structures, Frei Otto, and the English engineering team of BuroHappold.

The well-documented design and construction of the 3,100 square metre Expo 2000 *Japan Pavilion* heralded a new level of achievement for large-scale free-span architecture consisting primarily of a paper tube grid shell lattice. The innovative use of a double layer shell spliced together with flexible tape connections, enabled

left
Paper Loghouse
Kobe, Japan,
1994.
Paper tubes and tenting
material for roof.
52 m².
Courtesy Shigeru Ban
Architects.
Photo Takanobu Sakuma.

right
Paper Tea House
2008.
Paper tubes and
honeycomb cardboard.
Courtesy Shigeru Ban
Architects.

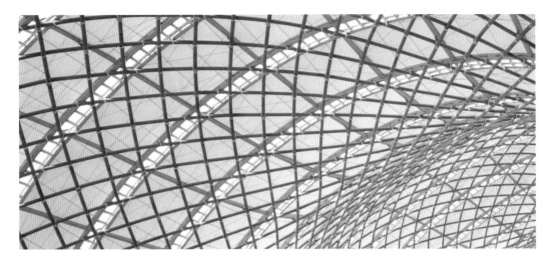

the complex, double-curved form to be accurately and quickly assembled, with the goal of achieving a completely recyclable building system.

Within the last few years, Ban has shifted his focus towards both simple, rapidly deployable disaster relief shelters made from cardboard tube frames, and also towards elegant and structurally efficient towers, sculptures and pedestrian bridges, meant to convey the strength, lightness and ecological sensitivity of cardboard as a building material. The 2009 London Design Festival tower, as well as the 2007 *Paper Bridge* and 2006 *Vasarely Pavilion*, both built in France, convey an increasing level of confidence and control of geometry, utilising paper tube structures.

While Ban is undoubtedly recognised as the leading proponent and pioneer of cardboard or paper tube architecture, the potential of this material has continued to attract attention from emerging architects, engineers and builders interested in alternative, ecologically sustainable materials. The Chinese architect Li Xinggang recently completed a hybrid cardboard tube and cardboard 'brick' temporary demonstration house for the Chinese Pavilion at the 2008 Venice Architecture Biennale. The project is proposed as an earthquake resistant, lightweight structure for everyday living, in response to the Great Sichuan earthquake in China.

Cardboard architecture may be seen, paradoxically, as both still in its infancy and also as a rapidly maturing, albeit experimental architecture, thanks to the pioneering work and research of Shigeru Ban, Frei Otto, and the less well known projects and experiments at the Delft University in the Netherlands by architects such as Mick Eekhout and Henk van Dijke. The future of an ecologically innovative architectural practice depends on the continuing efforts towards implementation of new forms and materials inspiring a new generation of architects to combine both the aesthetics of nature with its efficiency and economy of material. Cardboard is uniquely suited for this task, towards a lighter, more ecologically and socially responsive architecture.

1 Van Dooren, E and Van Iersal, T, *Cardboard Architecture*, Leiden: drukkerijGroen, 2006.
2 McQuaid, Matilda, *Shigeru Ban*, London: Phaidon Press, 2003, p. 14.

Japan Pavillion (detail)
2000.
Paper tubing.
Courtesy Shigeru Ban Architects.

Packaging Design

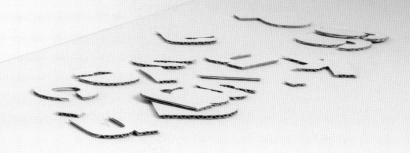

■ Initially conceived in light of nineteenth century packaging technology, cardboard has since become synonymous with packaging design, as the cardboard box remains the most recognised item of packaging in circulation today.

Cardboard's association with packaging design remains strong, no doubt on account of its cost, weight and potentiality for creating different shapes and sizes quickly and easily, as well as its blank surface on which branding and designs can be printed. It has, however, significantly developed since the day the cardboard box was invented, as designers increasingly concern themselves with ideas of recyclability, sustainability, practicality and originality in developing innovative new designs.

The following pages begin to explore various aspects of packaging design, from elementary designs used in food and drink packaging, to designs that have been conceived as packaging primarily, but can be re-used as products of some sort, such as GGRP's record sleeve, which doubles as a miniature human-operated record player; alongside are current reinterpretations, or 'improvements' on the humble cardboard box, such as Patrick Sung's Universal Packaging System.

Burgopak

Burgopak is an award-winning packaging design company whose patented slider packs and bespoke designs have been used by a range of leading brands around the world, including Motorola and Sony. Based in London and with five international offices, Burgopak's development of engaging opening mechanisms has become a design trait integral to the company's overall message—that packaging provides a tangible and interactive platform with which to connect brand and consumer, and encourage positive engagement through form and function. Their innovative approach to design and material choice is exemplified here in Bloomingdale's *Little Green Card* gift pack, which has been made from 70 per cent post-consumer material as part of an Earth Day promotion.

Bloomingdale's
Little Green Card
2010.
70 per cent post-
consumer material.
16 x 10 x 1 cm.
Courtesy Burgopak Ltd
and Bloomingdale's.

Jan Ctvrtnik

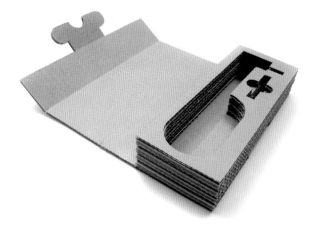

Jan Ctvrtnik's cardboard mobile phone packaging is made from a single sheet of folded and scored cardboard. The design follows a brief of creating an unexpensive, environmentally friendly box, which Ctvrtnik took one step further in creating this innovative packaging.

Ctvrtnik's portfolio of work covers a wide range of design disciplines, including furniture, jewellery, products, graphics, and packaging design. Born in the Czech Republic, Ctvrtnik has worked internationally, honing her design skills so that she is "able to bring innovative solutions to everyday life". She has also received numerous design awards in her home country, including, most notably, "Designer of the Year of the Czech Republic" in 2009.

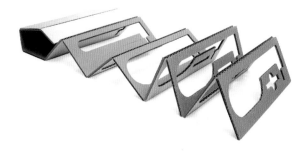

Harmonica
2008.
Courtesy Jan Ctvrtnik.

Conservation by Design Limited

Conservation by Design Limited's range of high quality storage products—including acid free boxes, safe transparent polyester album pages, acid free papers and museum boards—are all made from European, Japanese and Indian papers. The Green EcopHant Archive Boxes are made from a high density, hard pressed recycled cardboard, making the boxes stronger, longer lasting and apparently resistant to the effects of fire and floods. Each of the elegant green storage boxes have been embossed with "Made from reclaimed CXD acid free post-production material".

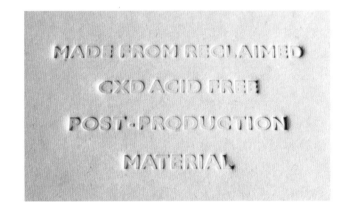

Green EcopHant
Archive Boxes
Acid and lignin free
recycled cardboard,
dimensions variable.

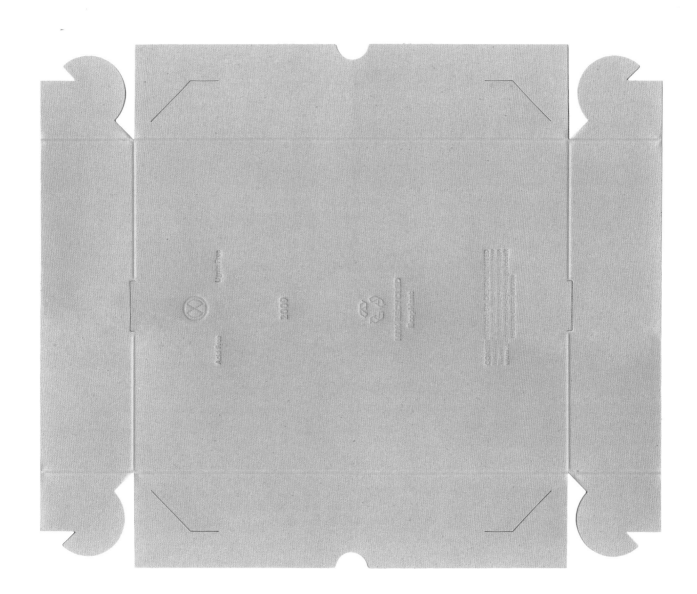

Gonsher Design

Ian Gonsher's work subverts the usual expectations of furniture design, using a range of materials in unique projects that elide reality and imagination, such as his Flowers Floating on Water, Floating on Air and his range of Displaced furniture, in which traditional wooden pieces are attached obliquely to a large perspex cube. His work in corrugated cardboard includes Adding value to the ubiquitous cardboard box, packaging-cum-furniture, which once pressed flat and cut, can be assembled to form a round-topped table. Red circular patterns on each face of the packaging add an additional aesthetic element to the design.

Ian Gonsher holds BFAs in Art History and Industrial Design. Before earning his MFA in Furniture Design from Rhode Island School of Design, he worked for Humberto and Fernando Campana, Bludot, and the Vitra Design Museum. He is currently on the faculty in the Department of Visual Art at Brown University., and his work has been featured in a number of design publications, including *1000 Ideas for Creative Reuse* and *Cool Green Stuff: A Guide to Finding Great Recycled, Sustainable, Renewable Objects You Will Love.*

Adding value to the
ubiquitous cardboard box
2004.
61 x 61 x 61 cm.
Courtesy Gonsher Design.

GGRP

GGRP's innovative Making it Make Noise record player is illustrative of their unique approach to sound engineering. The company, founded in 1968 in Vancouver, Canada, by Brian Griffiths, Brian Gibson and Miles Ramsay, was initially set up to produce jingles. GGRP's primary concern now lies away from jingle production—due to the advancement of television and radio advertising and the emergence of new web-based media—instead embracing various aspects of modern sound design, such as music production, voice directing, casting, music licensing, SFX technology, script writing and audio post-production.

Making it Make Noise encapsulates the company's progressive outlook. Ostensibly a conventional record sleeve made from corrugated cardboard, the envelope opens to form a miniature human-operated record player. Once assembled, a record can be spun on the player, by using a common pencil. The vibrations course through the needle and are amplified by the cardboard, whose corrugated inner and fibreboard outer layers project the vibrations. The players were sent out to creative directors across North America as a creative demonstration of GGRP's sound engineering capabilities.

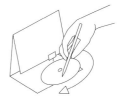

above and overleaf
Making it Make Noise
2010.
Courtesy GGRP.

Place the needle on the record. Spin the record using a pencil or stick.

Town THAT FOUND ITS SOUND
SIDE A
GORP SOUND
GORP.COM

Graphic Thought Facility

London-based design consultancy Graphic Thought Facility create print and digital graphics, products and environments for a range of clients. The MeBox is a unique cardboard packaging/storage system that on one end is covered in a grid of perforated, press-out discs, from which letters, numbers and symbols can be created. Intended for use in both the home and office, the MeBox is available in a range of silk-screened colours, all flat-packed for self-assembly.

MeBox
2002.
Perforated cardboard.
Courtesy Graphic
Thought Facility.

Julia

Created for Nexus Productions—a production and animation studio based in London and Paris—by Julia—a design agency, specialising in typographic work, the Showreel was conceived as a clever solution to the packaging system used to send their show reels on demand; the requirements being that the packaging encompassed both the DVD box and the envelope, whilst also being recyclable.

Made from corrugated cardboard—chosen for its lightness, resistance, flexibility and cost—the packaging opens by pulling down a perforated tear strip to reveal the director of the production's name. Within the multi-functioning packaging, the DVD and booklet are encased.

Showreel
2009.
Corrugated cardboard.
Courtesy Julia and
Nexus Productions.

Chris Waitt

Nexus Productions

Showreel

Matmo

Matmo is a Dutch multi-media design studio specialising in visual communication, and working within the fields of print, interaction, motion and environmental design. For the Dutch pavilion of the World Expo 2010 in Shanghai, Matmo created this food packaging design, commissioned by catering company Maison van den Boer, that gave an illustrative twist to the traditional image of The Netherlands.

Food packaging for
Maison van den Boer
2010.
Courtesy Matmo.

Élie Monge

This simple concept in CD casing was designed by Élie Monge in a packaging class at Université du Québec à Montréal as an alternative to the ubiquitous plastic jewel case. The particularly innovative aspect of the design, which sets it apart from much other cardboard CD packaging, is its use of a continuous, detachable strip to house the CDs. This has three obvious advantages, the first being that it allows total flexibility in the choice of number of CDs to be packaged together, which in turn reduces the amount of packaging per CD as the number of discs packaged together increases. The strip then folds together in a concertina-like way to a similar size and shape to a traditional plastic case, making it a space-saver, too. Its blank surfaces have the potential to be printed with a band's album artwork for commercial use, or simply left blank to be personalised and used for home DVDs and CDs. Made of recycled and recyclable cardboard, the sustainability credentials of this packaging far outweigh those of the plastic cases that dominate the market today without compromising on style.

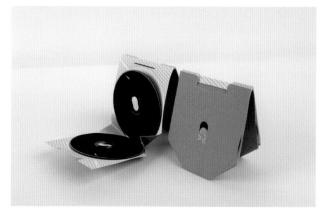

CD Packaging
2009.
Courtesy Élie Monge.

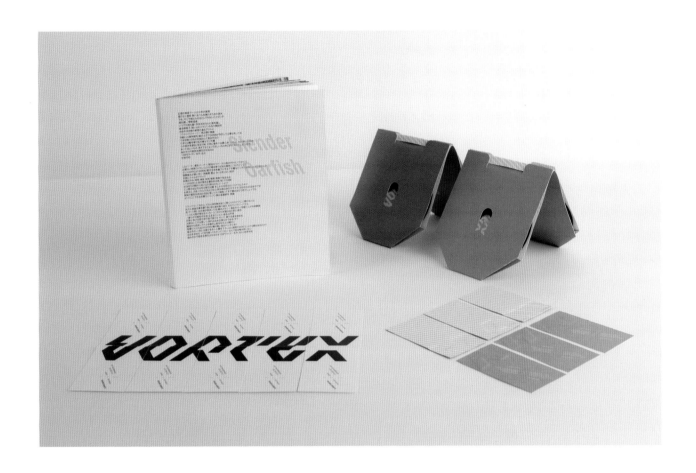

Patrick Sung

Patrick Sung's 2010 IF Concept award-winning UPACKS Universal Packaging System is a solution to the oft-encountered problem of finding the correct packaging for shipping irregularly shaped items. Inspired by Computer-Aided Design (CAD) programmes, the recyclable cardboard sheet features semi-perforated polygon patterns, allowing it to be folded to fit the item being shipped without compromising structural integrity or durability and allowing the sender to package the item correctly from the least material possible. Alternatively, while irregularly shaped items will not be able to be stacked, UPACKS can be folded into conventional cardboard box form; its versatility providing a more economical alternative to over-sized cardboard boxes.

Patrick Sung graduated from Emily Carr University of Art and Design, Vancouver, with a degree in Bachelor of Industrial Design in 2008. Since then he has developed his design philosophy that involves "finding creative solutions that improve the quality of the environment, while helping people to achieve their goals and improving quality of life through good design". From 2007 to 2009, he worked as a studio assistant at renowned paper design company Molo Design, helping to develop new products while redesigning packaging for their range of products, whilst simultaneously concentrating on his own designs.

UPACKS Universal
Packaging System
2008.
61 x 61 cm.
Courtesy Patrick Sung.

Tetra Pak

Founded in 1951 by Dr Reuben Rausing as a way to package liquids in order to maximise their longevity, Tetra Pak has since become one of the leading international food packaging companies.

Best known for the Tetra Classic, the tetrahedral packaging allows liquids to be packed in a vacuum and stored for up to one year, minimising use of materials and maximising hygiene. The Tetra Pak cartons use a compound of materials generally consisting of 73 per cent paperboard for strength and stability, 22 per cent plastic, and, depending on the package, five per cent aluminium. The plastic is used to coat the paperboard in layers on either side to give the packaging renewed strength and durability.

Tetra Pak's influence upon the packaging industry and innovative use of materials, has led to numerous different representations of the original design, that include experimental shapes and sizes and an array of different colours and prints.

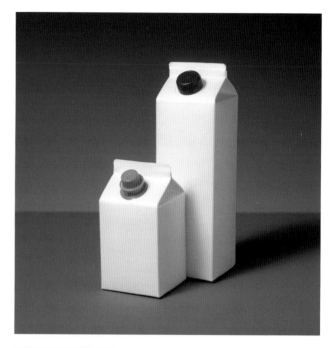

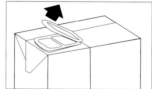
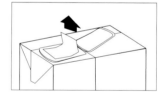

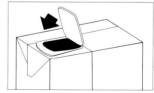

Tetra Pak
Courtesy Tetra Pak.

Raw Edges

Design studio Raw Edges, founded by Royal College of Art Product Design graduates Yael Mer and Shay Alkalay in 2007, have gained recognition for their range of products, from the bags and luggage designed for Chinese company Kobold in 2007, to 2006's British Council Student award-winning Milk Cartons, exhibited at the Talented: Graduates 2006 design festival in Milan.

Milk Cartons uniquely distinguishes between different levels of fat content in each variety of milk by the form of each pack, rather than colour. The length and taper of the folds on the front of each pack denote whole, skimmed or semi-skimmed milk and conceal the spout, which folds out from the top of the carton, with similar folds on the back acting as a handle with which to grip.

Since graduating, Raw Edges have received a number of reputable awards for design, including the 'IF' Gold Award and the Dutch Design Award, with work exhibited in the permanent collection of the Museum of Modern Art, New York (MoMA) and The Design Museum, London.

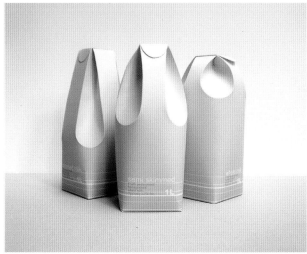

Milk Cartons
2006.
Courtesy Raw Edges.

Wewow

Wewow are a CD and DVD replication company with a deep concern for the way their products are packaged. Motivated by the environmental impact of traditional plastic packaging, the company have created an entire portfolio of eco-friendly packaging solutions under the name of WeEco. The innovative range avoids plastic completely in favour of using sustainable cardboard and other natural materials. Any inks used in printing the cardboard are vegetable-based, where possible, and the use of matt or gloss laminates is also avoided. Pictured here is the WowSpiral, originally designed for folk artist Peter Roe's EP *The Merry-Go-Round*, but now a staple of Wewow's packaging services. Its design embodies the company's principles of simple, creative, eco-friendly, and cost-effective packaging. The spiral's distinctive shape lends it a unique and pleasing aesthetic while comprising just one single piece of card, which folds to form a secure, spiral-shaped clasp. Not only does this minimise the amount of material used, but it also means that no glue is required to stick separate pieces together.

WowSpiral
2010.
Courtesy Wewow.

Zoo Studio

Barcelona based company Zoo Studio are a multi-faceted design firm whose portfolio of work includes packaging, web and corporate identity design. Their packaging design for the limited edition chocolate egg—*Huevo Código*, translating as *Code Egg*—by the chocolate artist Rubén Álvarez, is comprised of a neat cardboard box, within which a chocolate egg has been individually packaged. A label, each featuring a unique number or 'code' that has simultaneously been printed on the chocolate egg, and signed by Álvarez, is used to seal the box.

top, bottom and
overleaf
Huevo Código
(*Code Egg*)
2009.
Courtesy Zoo Studio.

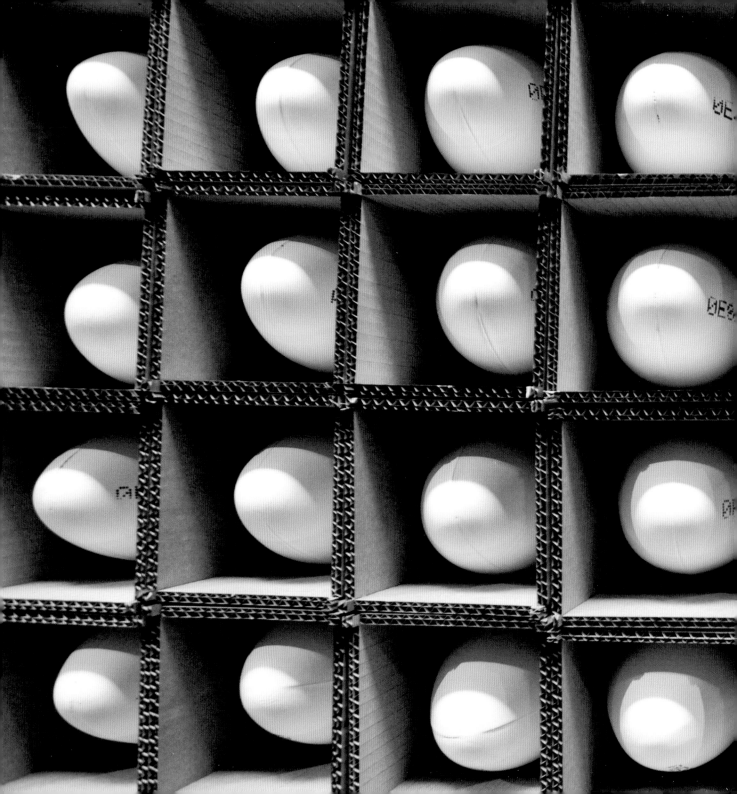

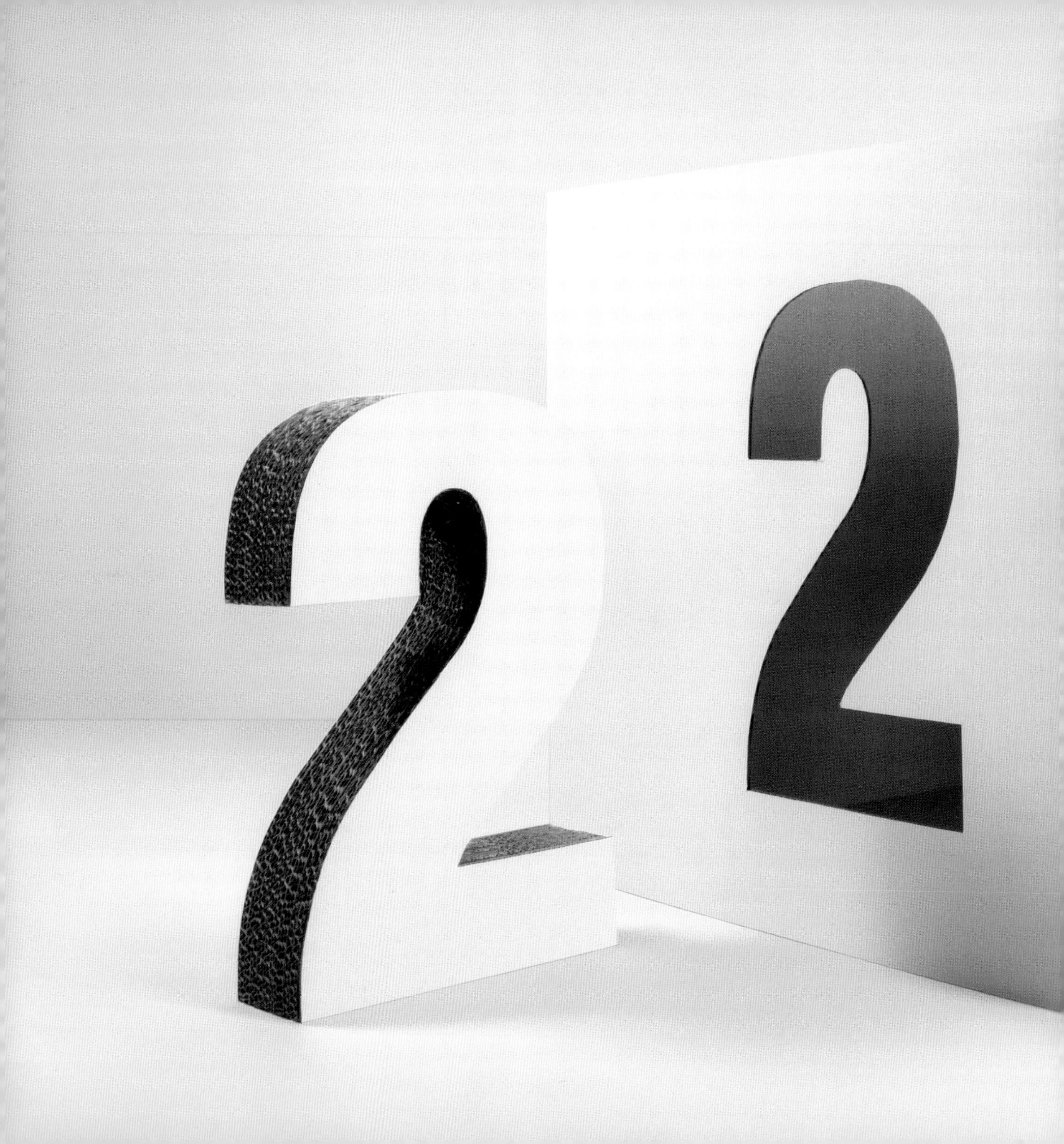
2
2

Product
Design

■ In recent years, cardboard's use in design has been preferably adopted by product designers who view the material's adaptability, cost, weight, and potential to recycle as increasingly attractive. An industry that concerns itself with the continual re-evaluation of 'products'—from kitchen utensils to laptop computers—it has in recent years shown a growing appreciation for the paper product, as an emphasis upon efficiency in relation to both manufacture and use has become central to the practice of designers working in the area.

From basic products, where cardboard is used as a cost-effective material, to expensive design items that highlight the material the product is made from as a distinctive feature—as demonstrated in Cardboardesign's range of Liquid Cardboard; the following chapter presents a range of items that highlight the malleability of the material, giving prevalence to the numerous possibilities in which it can be fashioned both aesthetically and practically.

From the portability of Muji's Cardboard Speakers, to the sustainability of Recompute by Houston-based designer Brenden Macaluso, and even to the texturally reliant products from d-torso and Giles Miller, who capitalise upon the roughly hewn edges of corrugated cardboard to create certain effects for which their products have become recognised; the following chapter presents the various different routes in which cardboard in product design has begun to take, and opens up suggestions to where it may subsequently lead.

A4A Design

Italian design firm A4A Design specialise in the production of design objects and furniture in honeycomb cardboard. Originally working as architects, A4A soon became accustomed to the creative use of cardboard through the industry. Within their wide remit of work, A4A produce cardboard stage settings, installations for exhibitions and commercial areas, and toys for children "creating urban designs with a strong aesthetic and social impact … exploit(ing) the fun side of cardboard".

Their innovative and exciting cardboard models for children consist of various interlocking cardboard parts that are intended to be built by the child to create different items including flowers, trees, animals and vehicles, in a myriad of shapes, colours and patterns—as seen in the Xmas tree and prickly pear. The Xmas tree is available in various different colours and sizes—from miniature to full-scale models, the latter of which can be used as an ecological alternative to the traditional Christmas tree.

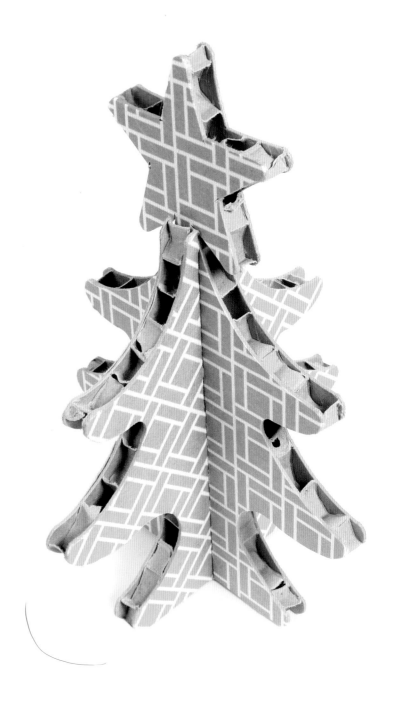

opposite top centre
flower (**small**)
20 x 29 cm.

right
Xmas tree (**small**)
20 x 29 cm.

opposite top right
apple tree
40 x 29 cm.

opposite top left
and bottom
prickly pear
40 x 29 cm.

All images courtesy
A4A Design.

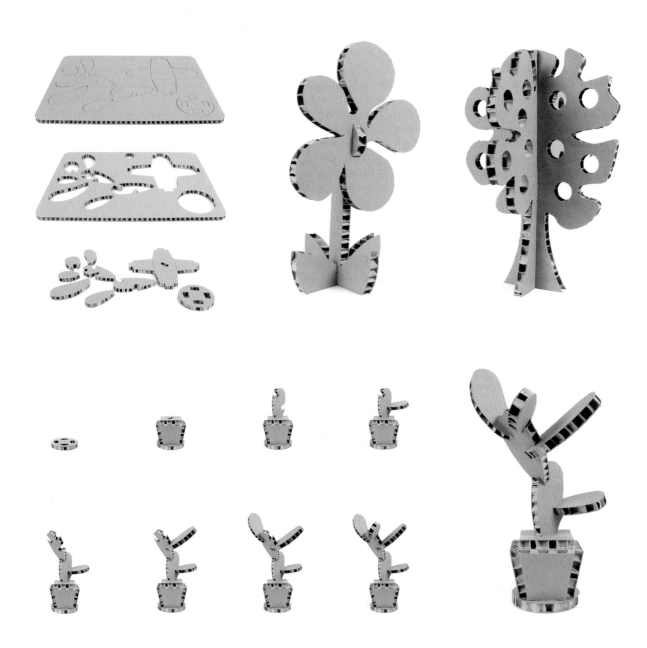

¿adónde?

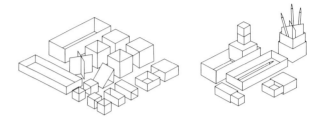

French design firm ¿adónde? pride themselves on their green credentials, with their cardboard products—Boîtes and Boîtes à lumière—being made using recycled cardboard and FSC certified coloured paper. Boîtes feature seven "do-it-yourself recycled cardboard boxes" which are intended to be used to hold stationary and other desktop items. Sold in many different colours, all depicted in a colour bar featured on their elegant brown paper packaging—evocative of the cardboard product within—alongside simple diagrams of the various uses and constructions possible with the cardboard templates. The firm's Boîtes à lumière—a fully functioning series of cardboard lamps—work on a similar premise as Boîtes, with their continuation of colours, and similarities in material, shape and construction; they also continue to promote the company's commitment to proving cardboard as a versatile material used in well-designed products.

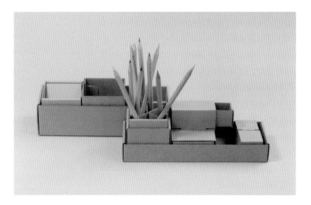

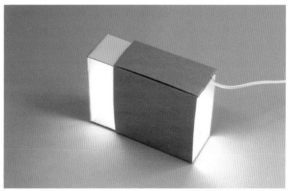

centre
Moutarde Boîtes
Recycled cardboard
and FSC certified
coloured paper.
23 x 7 x 8 cm.

bottom
Boîte à lumière
Recycled cardboard
and FSC certified
coloured paper.
17 x 17 x 7 cm.

opposite
Violet Boîtes
Recycled cardboard
and FSC certified
coloured paper.
23 x 7 x 8 cm.
All images
courtesy ¿adónde?.

Boites (assortment)
23 x 7 x 8 cm.
Courtesy ¿adónde?.

Calafant

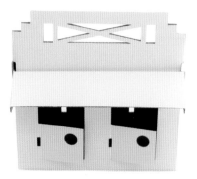

The Calafant "Cardboard Land of Fantasies" philosophy follows the motto of creating "smart toys for smart kids" by combining the passion and profession of the company's founder—cartoonist and packaging designer Boris Schimanski—for cartoons and cardboard. The range of flat packed models, which spans from small, easy to assemble vehicle designs aimed at smaller children, to more complex constructions such as the treehouse, focuses on the child's need for creative play, and offers them the joy of playing with a self-made toy. Every piece is made from pre-cut and pre-punched cardboard, enabling the models to be put together without glue or scissors, while the cardboard material used is specially produced for the company to ensure that the toys are sturdy, light and flexible enough for children to carry, throw, and push around without being damaged. The white surface can then be decorated according to imagination. Calfant's artistic creativity and extensive experience with cardboard materials are manifested in the little details evident in their designs, such as the bull's head motif on the doors of the fort model, which make the models attractive toys in themselves, not merely by virtue of the fun to be had when assembling them.

above and opposite
Fort
37 x 37 x 23 cm.
Courtesy Calafant.

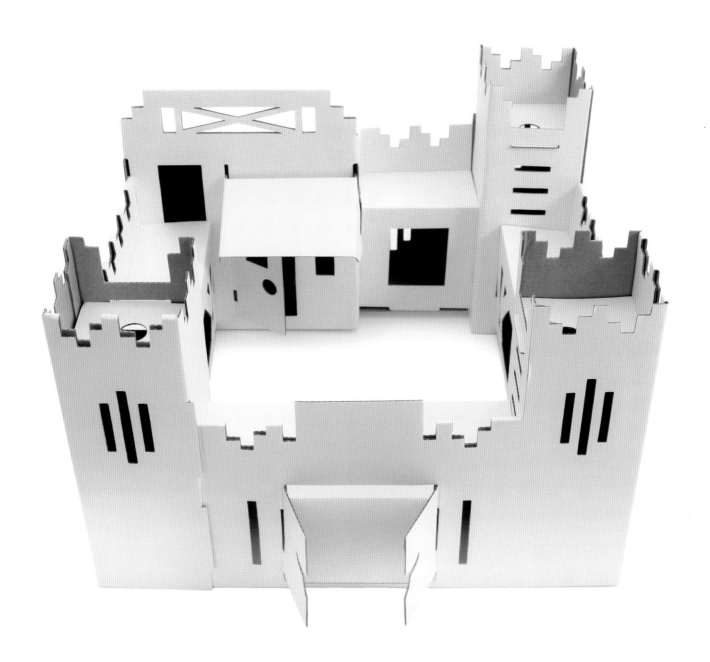

Cardboardesign

New York-based firm Cardboardesign are producers of environmentally friendly, chemical-free recyclable cardboard products—such as furniture, shelving, children's toys and vases. Among their more distinctive products is 'liquid cardboard', a range of visually-arresting ornaments capable of changing shape and manufactured solely of secondary fibre—such as corrugated cardboard containers, kraft paper and old newspapers; materials that otherwise would have become the contents of landfill.

Sharp and tactile, yet simultaneously fluid, Liquidcardboard's structure comprises thousands of concertinaed cells glued together and compressed in a honeycomb pattern that lends the cardboard the rigidity to keep its shape but also the flexibility to alter its form. It combines both function and aesthetic as a container for household objects and as a re-workable sculpture, which seeks to foster creativity and provide relief from stress. By manipulating the hole in the ornament's centre, it will assume an array of different solid forms when placed on a flat surface. Placing objects inside the liquid cardboard structures will produce more dramatic effects, whilst acting as a stabiliser on the new, less stable, sculpture.

The company's range of liquid cardboard pieces includes designs of different cuts and dimensions, which have been engineered to interact with each other and produce composite ornaments of even greater depth and complexity.

Liquidcardboard
Recycled cardboard.
Variable sizes.
Courtesy Cardboardesign.

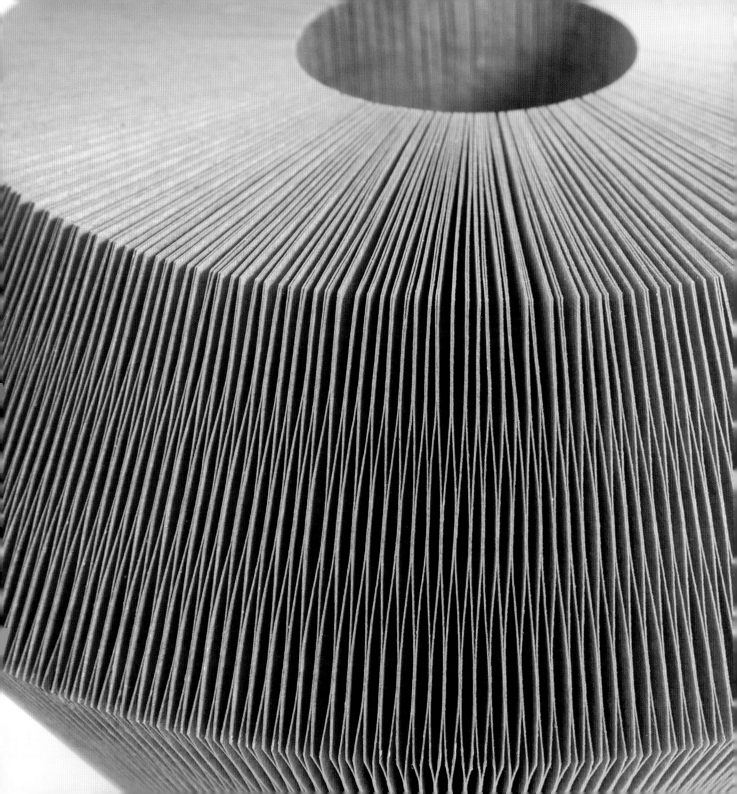

Liquidcardboard
Variable sizes.
Courtesy Cardboardesign.

d-torso

Aki Co. Ltd.'s d-torso system of laser-based figurative design and construction allows the deconstruction and rebuilding of three-dimensional forms by way of "slice data ... using three axes of coordinates". Aki Co. has created various products using this technique—from wine bottle holders to full size mannequins—but in this case, it has been appropriated to create intricate three-dimensional body-models of different animals from slim sheets of corrugated cardboard. The models appear almost academic in their detail and expressiveness, and are incredibly sturdy and complex considering their construction material—a result of the use of laser-cutting in creating the piece's constituent parts.

right
Giraffe (**illustration from instructions**)
12 x 17 x 33 cm.

opposite top and
bottom left
Rhino
Cardboard and paper.
16 x 9 x 5 cm.

opposite bottom right
Chihuahua
3.5 x 11 x 10 cm.

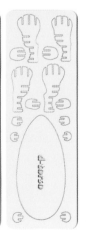

Charles Eames

Conceptualised to celebrate "familiar and nostalgic objects from the animal, mineral and vegetable kingdoms"—those things that the designer Charles Eames considered "the good stuff"— the Eames House of Cards, originally designed in 1952, is a set of oversized toy playing cards—each measuring approximately 4.5 x 7 inches—with incorporated slots for structural building. The cards, which were originally supplied as two 54-card "Picture" and "Pattern" decks, feature a mix of object images such as vegetables, cotton reels, fish and buttons, and more abstract patterns, with the ubiquitous Eames star symbol on the reverse.

Charles Eames, along with his brother Ray, was a well known twentieth century American designer, who largely specialised in modern architecture and furniture, as well as producing a number of films about their work and interests.

House of Cards
1952.
8-ply cardboard.
11 x 17 cm.

Kidsonroof

By their own admissions "Kidsonroof = creativity + imagination + sustainable approach = great to play with -/- visual pollution for the grown ups". Their range of cardboard products and furniture is a bid by the company to offer ecological design options to the children's market.

Their Totem collection is a range of colourful cardboard models, sold in sturdy cardboard boxes, which when opened reveal the flat-packed pieces, depicted in a multitude of reversible patterns. The Totem's are constructed by slotting each piece into place without the need for any tools or glue, each of which is printed with a design reminiscent of the Totem's theme. The series includes Totem Mini Rooster—a basic model, ideal for young children; Totem City—featuring a church, an aeroplane, a ship and a 'yak'; and Totem Nature—featuring a lizard, a deer, a church and a 'witchhouse'.

Kidsonroof's MobileHome is a portable dolls house for "knights, pirates and princesses" that features eight rooms, stair openings and 'spyholes', sold in a variety of colours and patterns including white, blue and Recycle! green.

above
Mobile Home White
46 x 23 x 36 cm.

opposite left
Totem City: Vessel
2009.
Recycled cardboard.

opposite right
Totem Nature: Lizard
2009.
Recycled cardboard.

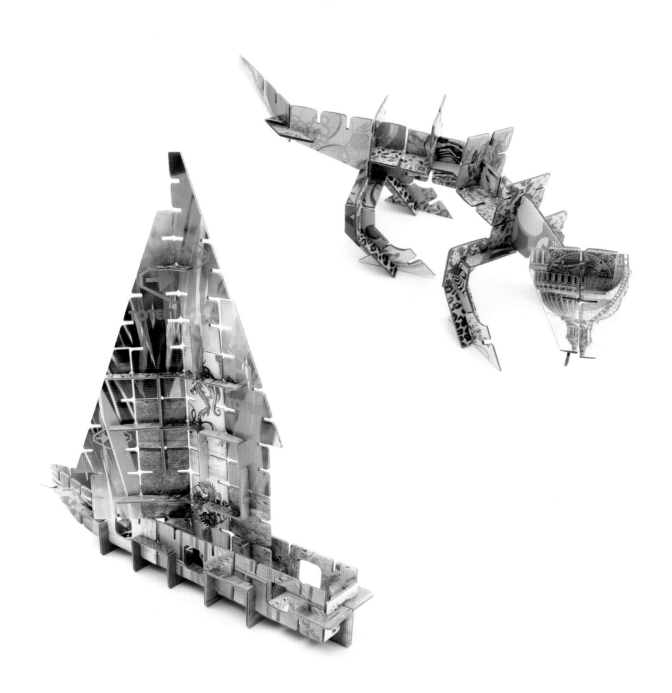

PRODUCT DESIGN • 69

Kikkerland

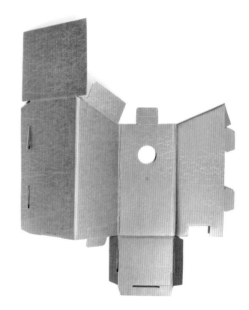

American design firm Kikkerland pride themselves on making "smart things that make everyday tasks easier. And gentle things that make you feel happier when you use them". Their foldable birdhouse is sold flat packed and is intended to be assembled at home, without the need for any tools or glue. Fully water repellent, the birdhouse is supposed to withstand being left outside in all weather conditions; it also comes with a wood dowel to provide a sturdy front perch for the birds. Kikkerland encourage the customer to decorate the birdhouse using pens, markers and stickers.

Foldable birdhouse
31 x 16 cm.
Courtesy Kikkerland.

Brenden Macaluso

Recompute is a fully functioning PC, which houses exclusively off-the-shelf components, including an Intel Core 2 Duo CPU and 2GB of RAM, in a corrugated cardboard outer shell. Houston-based designer Brenden Macaluso hit upon the viability of cardboard as a casing material for his sustainable computer in order to alleviate a host of environmental problems precipitated by the production of computer parts and their eventual disposal by the consumer.

Easily recyclable, Macaluso argues that cardboard is a more suitable material for building computer components, as the average PC operates for only approximately four or five years before being discarded.

Despite retorts to its suitability as a material for containing heat-radiating parts, cardboard is more heat-resistant than many plastics, with much higher points of fire and ignition—258°C and 427°C, respectively—than plastic, which begin to melt at around 120°C. Moreover, Recompute's cardboard composition is but one facet of its sustainability: implicit in its design is the reduced manpower, parts and harmful processes required for its construction, with the additional benefit that nearly all of each computer can be recycled.

Recompute is an emphatic rebuke to modern industrial processes, an unlikely paragon for the use of organic materials in modern technology design.

above and overleaf
Recompute
2008.
43 x 18 x 28 cm.
Courtesy Brenden Macaluso.

Enzo Mari

One of Italy's most influential designers of the late twentieth century, Enzo Mari has collaborated with various companies, including Danese and Alessi. Concerned with ideas of perception and communication, his product design-orientated work naturally evolved to include games and puzzles for children, motivated by the linguistic analysis of communication. *Il Gioco dell Favole*, translating as The Fable Game, was created by Mari in 1965 and consists of twelve pieces that slot together to depict various carefully detailed images of animals (45 to be exact), objects, plants, the sun and moon—all of which are featured in popular fairy tales and fables. By arranging the cards in different formations the child is able to narrate imaginative stories according to their order.

The Fable Game
1965.
Now published by
Corraini Edizioni.
Copyright Enzo Mari.
Courtesy Corraini Edizioni.

Giles Miller

Giles Miller first started seriously experimenting with corrugated cardboard over a year of independent experimentation after graduating from studying Furniture Design at Loughborough University in 2006. Following his graduation from the Product Design masters at the Royal College of Art in 2009, Miller has continued to expand his portfolio and his range of corrugated cardboard products, utilising similarly unconventional materials to create unique new furniture, such as his Hirsutio vase, constructed from finely-cut aluminium and brass.

Miller's cardboard range reveals his consideration for sustainability in design. His 2010 residency at the London Design festival—Giles Miller at Kingly Court—displayed his stunning array of cardboard furniture, encapsulating his sensitivity to sustainability and his distress at the escalation of environmentally damaging materials in modern design. Miller utilises a unique 'fluting' process, which enables him to manipulate the intrinsic structure of corrugated cardboard into hitherto unachievable shapes and patterns. His cardboard lamps and screens feature rich, variegated floral motifs. When the lamp is illuminated, incandescent light shimmers between the layers of paperboard and inner corrugation, creating contrast between each motif and the blank cardboard background.

left to right
Flute Screens
2006.
Corrugated cardboard.
120 x 40 x 170 cm.

Exbox Bench
2005.
Corrugated cardboard.
100 x 100 x variable
lengths.

Cardcase
2006.
Corrugated cardboard,
leather, chrome buckles.
33 x 38 x 43 cm.

Fric Floor Lamp
2007.
Corrugated cardboard
shade, powder coated
steel stand.
46 x 46 x 160 cm.

Brown Paper Handbag
2007.
Corrugated cardboard,
leather, chrome buckles.
21 x 26 x 27 cm.

opposite clockwise
from top left
Flute Lamp (**small**)
2007.
Corrugated cardboard.
26 x 26 x 40 cm.

Mantle Clock-C
2009.
Corrugated cardboard.

Fric Floor Lamp
2007.
Corrugated cardboard
shade, powder coated
steel stand.
46 x 46 x 160 cm.
All images Courtesy
Giles Miller.

Mitik

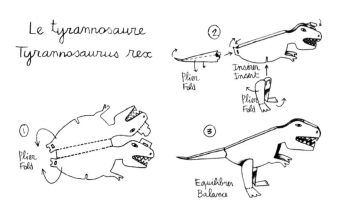

French company Mitik, founded by Myriam Tiberghien, creates imaginative children's toys, with an underlying aim of developing a child's confidence through artistic expression, achieved through their construction of the models, and eventual decoration.

Mitik's products are all made from 100 per cent recycled cardboard and include various ranges of self-construct toys. Dinodulos consists of 12 pre-cut white cardboard dinosaurs: a Diplodocus, Triceratops, T-Rex, three Fabrosorus, a Stegosaur, two Pterodactyls, two Ouranosaurus, and an Ankylosaurus, all of which are sold flat-packed ready to be assembled and painted. Much the same, Animodulos feature 15 self-construct cardboard animals.

Mask Animo is a set of eight animal masks made from paperboard, ready to assemble and paint in the customers chosen colours and patterns. The colourful cast of animals available with Mask Animo include Charlie the dog, Corentine the chicken, Frida the cow, James the pig, Garviy the fox, Pablo the cockerel, Pedro the wolf and Brummi the bear. Each mask is worn using lengths of elastic to keep them in place.

An improvement on the paper plane, Mes Z'Avions features three sturdy cardboard models of planes. Sold flat-packed, the planes are to be constructed by the customer and personalised with various accessories and stickers, ready to be launched by hand.

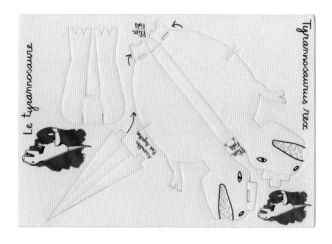

above
Dinodulos:
Tyrannosaurus Rex
Recycled cardboard
flat-packed.

opposite top left
Animodulos: Sheep
Recycled cardboard.
37 x 26 cm.

opposite bottom left
Animodulos: Rabbit
Recycled cardboard.
37 x 26 cm.

opposite top right
Dinodulos: Diplodocus
Recycled cardboard.
37 x 26 x 2 cm.

opposite bottom right
Dinodulos:
Tyrannosaurus Rex
Recycled cardboard.
37 x 26 x 2 cm.

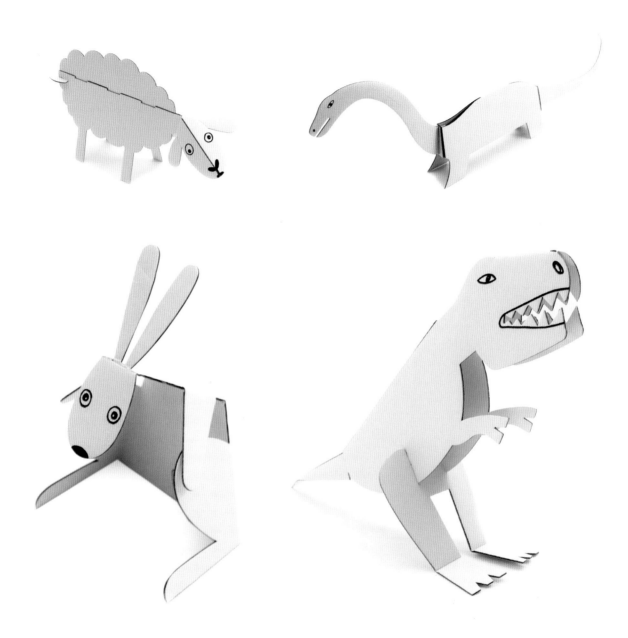

Mr Kaliski

After studying sculpture at the Royal College of Art, Mr Kaliski began to develop a range of products and furniture that included his cardboard Billy Rocker—an abstract rocking horse for children that can be imagined as various different animals.

"An environmentally sound product that bridges the gap between plastic and wooden toys" the Billy Rocker is made from recycled cardboard as well as priding itself upon being fully recyclable once outgrown by its owner. Sold flat-packed, the Billy Rocker's blank surface is intended be decorated by the child to "encourage role-play and stimulate your child's imagination". Furthermore, Mr Kaliski's choice of material and its lightweight quality also lends itself to the child's safety when playing upon the rocker.

Billy Rocker
71 x 45 x 37 cm.
Courtesy Mr Kaliski.

Muji Animals

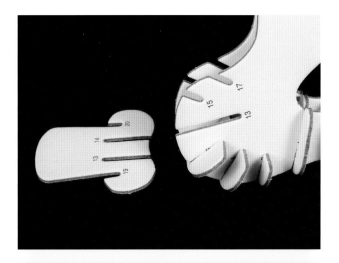

Like d-torso's similar laser-cut models, Muji's cardboard animals—created in collaboration with the Born Free Foundation for wildlife conservation—are both complex in their construction but also decidedly simple in their make up. By using over 60 constituent flat, cut-out parts, the model is afforded an almost skeletal appearance, but one which is also imposing and solid. The choice of animals that can be made—a dodo, a gorilla, and a mammoth, all supplied with information pertaining to their previous or prospective extinction— particularly lend themselves to these thicker structures, unlike the more waif-like choices for the d-torso figures.

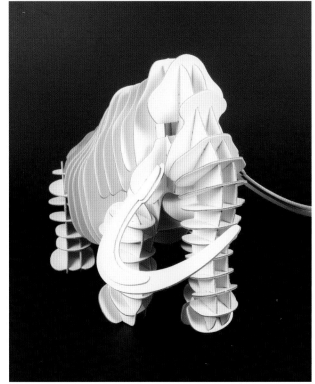

opposite and top
Cardboard Dodo

bottom
Cardboard Mammoth

overleaf
Cardboard Gorilla

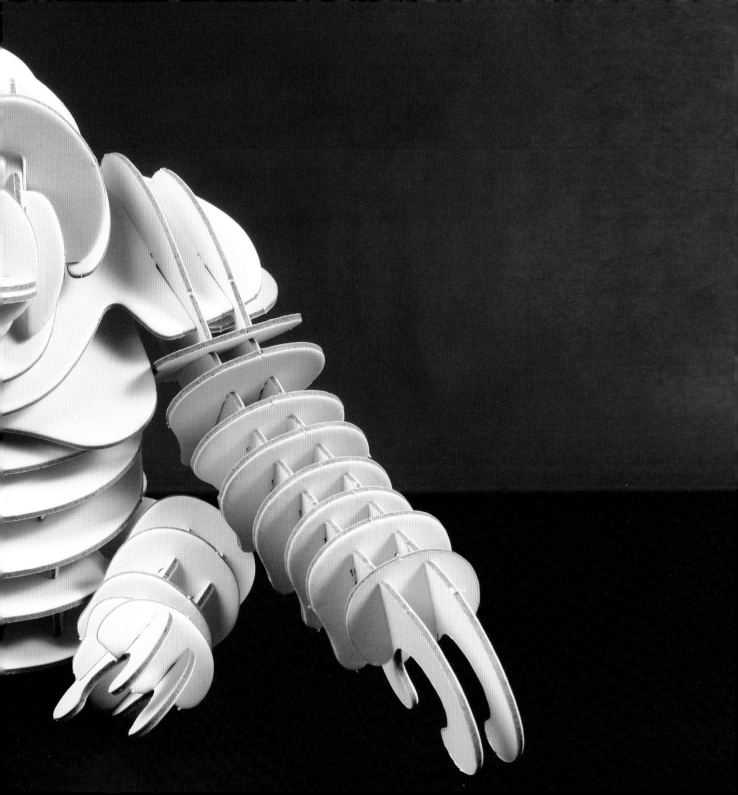

Muji
Postcards

Muji's cityscape greeting cards of London, New York and Paris come folded flat but, by use of a rudimentary five-layer pop-up system, attain a simple—though dense—3-D effect.

The cards depict various contemporary landmarks from each location: London foregrounds Tower Bridge against the Gherkin, Tate Modern and the Houses of Parliament, amongst others; New York sees the Statue of Liberty towered over by the Empire State and Chrysler buildings; and the Paris card sees the Eiffel Tower, the Arc De Triomphe and Notre Dame cathedral represented as paper silhouettes.

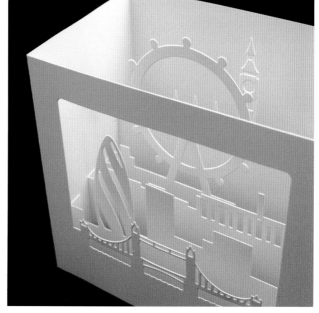

Postcard
11 x 13 x 10 cm.

Muji Speakers

Muji—the Japanese retailer founded in 1980, which now has stores in over 180 global locations—specialises in minimalist home-product design and clothing that is instantly recognisable for its clean, stark design and packaging.

The company's fold-up Cardboard Speaker is a perfect example of Muji's approach to their given aesthetic. The system comprises two small passive speaker units within rigid cardboard carton-style boxes, which can be constructed and destructed, and are packaged within a matt plastic zip wallet for easy portability.

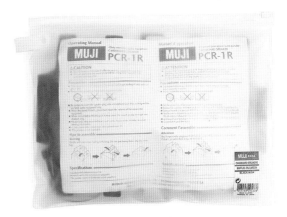

Cardboard Speaker
8 x 9 x 8 cm.

Joji Okazaki

The Japanese designer and artist Joji Okazaki came up with Atomic Bonzai in 1997, as a no-maintenance alternative to real-life bonsai trees. The DIY tree—which comes in packaging autographed by the artist—is made from 100 per cent recycled paper and non-toxic ink, and is manufactured by Smoggy Mountain in Los Angeles, California. The possible combinations for tree design afforded by the kit are almost endless, and the owner can effectively 'grow' their tree at whatever rate they prefer.

The popularity of the Atomic Bonzai kit—which has attracted impressively global press and coverage for Okazaki, who also known for his digital art and t-shirt design, and has created animations for TV shows such as Nickelodeon's *Hey Gabba Gabba*—has even led to its design being cheaply emulated by a well-known US home retailer.

Atomic Bonzai
18 x 18 cm.

P-Sharan

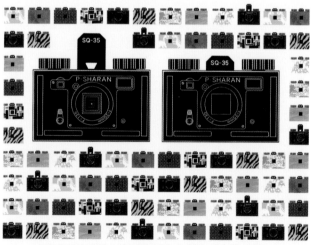

Sharan's distinctive pinhole cameras comprise sturdy, light-proof clamshell cardboard casing—though with plastic spools—and are assembled by hand without the need of cutting or glue. As well as a standard format model—the STD-35—the Japanese company also produces these square-format and panoramic designs, which also use standard 35mm film stock.

The SQ-35 has four image settings—standard, soft focus, and starburst settings for both—with two apertures and a soft-focus filter, whilst the Wide-35 produces panoramic 6.3 x 2.5 cm photographs. Despite the cameras' rudimentary appearances—the SQ-35 is partly help together by way of two elastic bands—the images produced retain a classic, washed out aesthetic of an alluringly ramshackle quality.

P-SHARAN SQ-35 PINHOLE CAMERA
35mm ピンホールカメラ紙製組立キット
SQUARE FORMAT – FOUR SETTINGS

EIGHT STICKERS INCLUDED TO CUSTOMIZE CAMERA

right
Sharan SQ-35
Cardboard and plastic.
10 x 7 x 3 cm.

opposite
Sharan Wide-35
Cardboard and plastic.
14 x 7 x 4 cm.

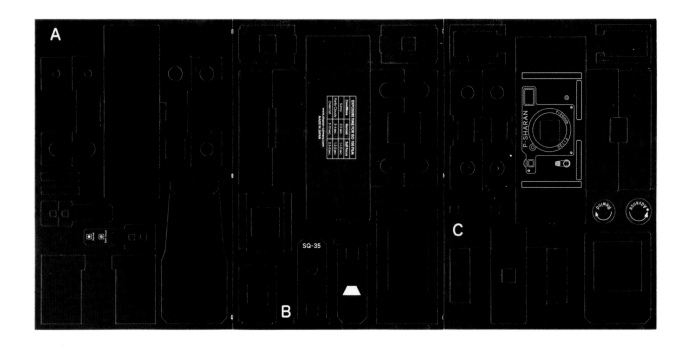

 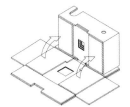 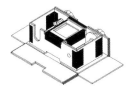 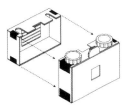

P-Sharan camera
Pinhole self-assembly,
flat-pack camera.

Paperpod

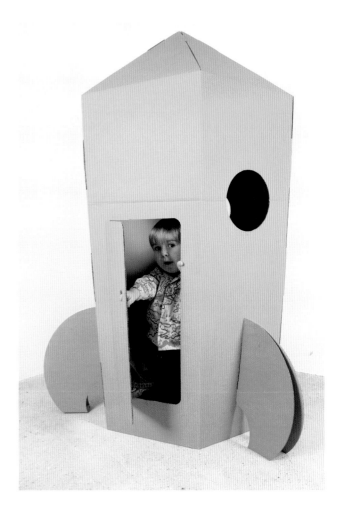

The Paperpod Rocket, characterised by the simplicity of its design, offers an alternative to "faddish, overpriced toys which are soon disposed of". The owner of the Sussex based company—award-winning product designer Paul Martin—has drawn on over 25 years of experience as a cardboard engineer to create a range of environmentally friendly, cost effective and practical toys to encourage children to engage in role-play and stimulate their imagination. Inspired by children discarding their expensive presents in favour of playing with the box they came in, Paperpod designs offer children a toy that is limited only by their own imagination. The product is flat-packed, ready for assembly, and made from recycled corrugated cardboard, offering the user a blank canvas which they can decorate with paints, crayons, or collage. The effectiveness of the Rocket as a toy is thus threefold, working respectively as a construction toy during assembly, as a craft toy for its decoration, and as a purposeful play structure as the end product. Once assembled, this beautifully simple product provides a safe, sturdy, and fun structure for children to play in, but can also be folded flat to be stored away when not in use.

Rocket
70 x 70 x 170 cm.

Postcarden

Postcarden—a renovation of the traditional greetings card—by London-based company A Studio for Design combines both card and gift within their innovative designs that open up into miniature cress gardens. Intricate and charming, each card is constructed using clever cuts and folds to enable the cress to interact fully with the scenery, producing a living, growing tableau.

With various designs made by a different British artist, each Postcarden comprises a three-dimensional cardboard pop-out scene, and an inner tray containing cress seeds which, when watered, grow into a fully edible cress plant. Like the traditional greetings card, the Postcarden allows space for the recipient's address and for the sender's greetings and can easily be sent in the post.

Botanical Carden
16 x 2 x 10 cm.

Push
For Pull

Push For Pull/Loona Goupe's distinctive DIY pinhole camera—designed to look like a more complex SLR—comprises over 40 separate pieces and is made completely of cardboard, aside from the miniscule metal pinhole aperture provided. The process of construction is, inevitably, quite exhaustive; and unlike Sharan's similar model—which has numerous plastic components within it's casing—the Hole-On Ex requires extensive rolling and gluing of parts.

By using an average exposure time of four seconds—controlled by moving the rudimentary "ON/OFF" tab within the 'lens'—one can create retro wide-angle, soft-focus images with no clearly discernible depth of field. The camera is marketed both as an effective way of introducing children to creative photography, and also as a cheap way to experiment with basic manual photographic techniques.

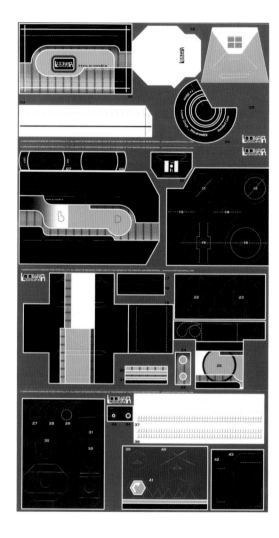

Hole-On Ex:
Make & Shoot
Pinhole camera
2007.
5 x 10 x 7 cm.

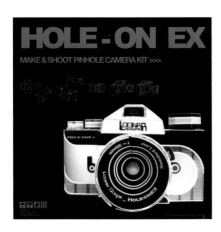

Judy Robinson

Judy Robinson is a London-based graphic designer and artist, originally from Melbourne, Australia. Having moved to London after completing a degree in Visual Communication, she established PaperTango, a company specialising in origami inspired gifts and greeting cards.

Using a technique pioneered by Japanese artist Masahiro Chatani, Robinson has created a range of two and three-dimensional pop-up cards featuring famous London landmarks, including Buckingham Palace, the London Eye and St. Stephen's Tower. Each representation pops up at a 90-degree angle and is made entirely from one sheet of A5 paperboard laser-cut and folded to render an exquisitely detailed miniature of the full-size landmark.

right
Opera House Card
Variable dimensions.

opposite
Big Ben Card
Variable dimensions.

Junzo Terada

Junzo Terada's Magical Menagerie is a collection of 20 punch-out animal models, realised in the artist's vintage, whimsical style. Terada, a Japanese artist and graphic designer—whose style bears comparison to individuals such as Shinzi Katoh and the British design company Sukie—utilises a plethora of muted patterns to block out the animal's bodies, affording a kind of 'seventies-wallpaper' aesthetic to his creations, which is both nostalgically comforting and visually idiosyncratic. The animals are sold in a sturdy cardboard box that continues the eclectic patterning of the models. Inside, along with the flat-packed animals, are colourful envelopes that allow the models to be posted to friends as a unique gift. The Magical Menagerie animals include a bear, kangaroo and seal, amongst many others.

right, opposite and
overleaf
Magical Menagerie
2009.
Variable dimensions.

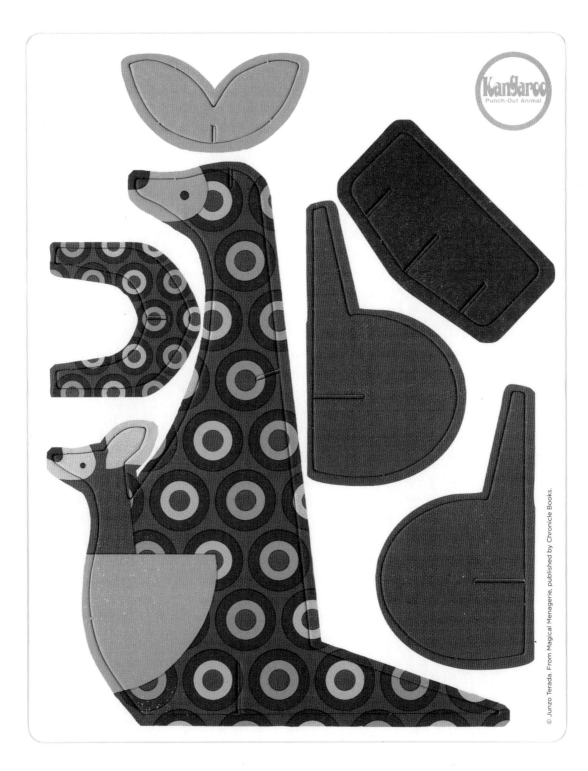

The Design Office

The Design Office is a collective of designers, each with a personal commission (alone or in collaboration with others). The members also develop projects without commission for various means of distribution and, as well as design projects, the company actively accumulates a collection of web and physical resources for use by members and guests of the Design Office facility. The design team comprises four members working full-time, with a number of occasional part-time members and production members.

Letter Boxes, made from corrugated cardboard have been designed to be a low cost, interactive kids toy. The four-inch cubes may be viewed and stacked from any direction, creating a plethora of unusual shapes and letters. The oversized kraft boxes reintroduce the alphabet not as 26 distinct letters, but as a combination of geometric parts, and allow for creativity by experimentation with these different letter patterns.

The boxes are made from recycled cardboard and delivered in flat-packed form, for ease of transport and for assembly by the customer. The company are still seeking manufacturing and distribution partners and the prototype is available for exhibit.

Letter Boxes
Corrugated cardboard.
10 x 10 cm.
Courtesy John Caserta
and Jeremy Mickel.

Furniture

■ Furniture designers' preference for using cardboard has become increasingly apparent within recent years. Its experimental appeal, surprising durability when layered or combined with other materials, and association with sustainable design, has created a plethora of possibilities for this often overlooked material.

From basic children's furniture designed with the expectation of being grown out of within a year, to 'flat pack' furniture intended for occasional or temporary use, alongside 'high-end' complex design items; this chapter explores the growing popularity of a material that has, until fairly recently, been solely used for the storage and transportation of items such as those displayed over the following pages.

These entries include the clean lines and minimalist design of Cardboard Future's Paperweight Desk, and the iconic Wiggle Chair by Frank Gehry—the latter of which can be considered, to some extent, as sparking a trend for the use of cardboard in furniture design—alongside WEmake's "designer furniture system" that encourages the customer to make their own cardboard furniture, and much more. This chapter disengages from the predisposition that cardboard is neither strong enough or durable enough to withstand the needs of everyday furniture, instead presenting a wealth of possibilities for the material's use.

Cardboard Future

Cardboard Future's Paperweight Desk is the first in a series of mass-produced cardboard furniture for the home and office that is set to include storage, book shelves, wardrobes and beds in a range of elegantly designed, minimalist shapes, sizes and colours, all of which show surprising strength.

Specially made from corrugated cardboard that has been coated with water-resistant cellulose varnish, the desk can be assembled without screws, staples, glues or tools, on average in around three minutes.

Priding themselves on being 100 per cent sustainable and recyclable, Cardboard Future's products are made from 76 per cent recycled paperboard, with the remainder being sourced from 100 per cent certificated sustainable raw materials from the UK and Europe. Also, wherever possible, the company takes back damaged or end-of-life products, donating them for the refurbishment of schools, nurseries, prisons and hospitals.

Paperweight Desk
2010.
Double walled
corrugated cardboard.
150 x 75 x 72 cm.
Courtesy Cardboard Future.

Carl Clerkin

Carl Clerkin's remake of Ernest Race and Isokon's classic Penguin Mark 2 Donkey was the designer's contribution to TEN XYZ for the 100% Design exhibition, London: "An exploration of… varied perspectives on the complex issues of sustainability within design, using digital manufacturing technologies."

Each member of the collective entered into a discussion on sustainability via designs for three-dimensional objects, which were then brought to life with the help of software and digital manufacturing technologies. With the help of creative industries centre Metropolitan Works, designers were given access to a range of technology and expertise to help produce their designs—including laser cutters, stereolithographs, water jet profilers and CNC routing machines—in a self proclaimed "return to the more concept driven framework of the original TEN in 2006".

A range of contributions were made to TEN XYZ dealing with different issues—Carl Clerkin's was that of designing with sustainable materials, whilst other contributions to the exhibition included utilising reclaimed and off-cut materials, combining digital technologies with found objects and materials, and the longevity of objects.

Through each of these projects and the wider discussion, TEN were attempting to highlight the problem of green-washing within the eco-design world.

Cardboard Copy
(Digital Donkey)
2009.
Corrugated cardboard.
40 x 53 x 40 cm.
Courtesy Carl Clerkin.

Cool Cardboard Furniture

A colourful contribution to cardboard design, Cool Cardboard Furniture specialises in handmade cardboard chairs for children and adults, constructed using either double corrugated cardboard or a densely sandwiched cardboard structure—90 per cent of which is recycled— which is then covered in handmade lotka paper, imported from India. Each item is bespoke in that the customer chooses the paper in which they would like their chair to be covered—the company's website showcasing myriad colours and patterns.

Cool Cardboard Furniture has been finished with a water based eco-varnish to ensure each item remains waterproof, whilst also providing durability. The company also prizes themselves upon their sustainability focus— most notably their emphasis upon the use of recycled materials in their products, alongside the opportunity to recycle the product once finished with its use.

top

Space Invader Stool
(**small**)
Double corrugated
cardboard, handmade
paper, varnish.
31 x 26 x 26 cm.

Space Invader Stool
(**large**)
Double corrugated
cardboard, handmade
paper, varnish.
44 x 38 x 32 cm.

bottom
Range of Cool Cardboard
Furniture, from left to
right: *Space Invader
Stool*; *Lozenge Chair*;
Art Deco Chair; *Space
Invader Stool*
All images courtesy
Stuart Knox.

Reinhard Dienes

German designer Rienhard Dienes' furniture possesses a playful nature, with its gentle angles, selection of vivid colours and witty features such as the Dickens Bookshelf's slanting shelf.

Both the bookcases and sideboards are fully recyclable corrugated cardboard plies, compressed to form a sturdy, yet lightweight, structure. Gentle perpendicular angles and a variety of shelving widths convey a sense of space and simplicity, comfortably accommodating both slim paperbacks and weighty tomes.

Rienhard Dienes has received wide acclaim in the international design community, receiving a nomination for the 2010 German National Design Award; coming second in the 2009 11° China Furniture Design Award; and winning the 'Living' category at annual Belgian design fair Interieur in 2008. He has also held teaching posts at the Academy of Arts and Design, Offenbach, since 2008, whilst also establishing a private studio in 2006.

right
Dickens Bookshelf
2010.
Corrugated cardboard.
150 x 55 cm.

opposite
Georgia Sideboard
2010.
Corrugated cardboard.
60 x 120 cm.
All images courtesy
Reinhard Dienes.

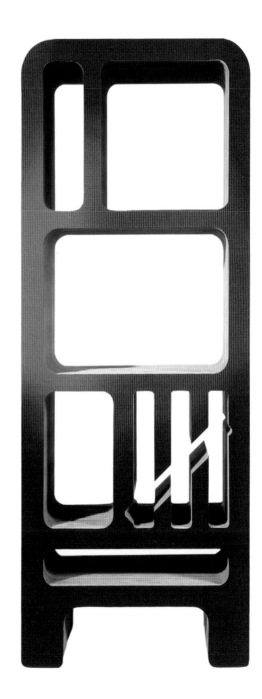

EUG Studio

EUG Studio are a London based product design/art direction studio founded in 1997 by Roberto Feo and Rosario Hurtado. Renowned for their large-scale installations and innovative reinvention of everyday products, Feo and Hurtado encourage the customer to redefine their preconceptions of a product's use and potential possibilities. It is this creative questioning of norms that can be thanked for the studio's international recognition, alongside Feo's and Hurtado's teaching appointments at both the Royal College of Art and Goldsmith's University.

EUG's lightweight cardboard and resin furniture series, previously exhibited at the Aram Gallery, London, pays homage to the company's design mantra, creating a permanent dining table from used cardboard, tape and resin. This composition of materials surprisingly gives the now permanent dining tables a 'structural ingenuity' not previously attributed to cardboard, and thanks to Feo and Hurtado's design know-how turns these brightly coloured tables into coveted design items. EUG distinguish their work as reflecting "upon their interest in how contemporary culture incorporates, re-uses and re-interprets the systems and structures that it has inherited. Within this context the challenge is to create new objects, which can be typologically disentangled from our conventional—learned—understanding of the world, and thus offer alternative ways to live, work and communicate."

above and opposite
Cardboard Tables
2009–2010.
Cardboard and resin.
Dimensions variable.
Courtesy EUG Studio.

Che Eyzenbach

Dutch designer Che Eyzenbach uses cardboard to express his fascination with organic and mathematical patterns. Eyzenbach's Flow—created for the designer's graduation from the Design Academy, Eindhoven—explores the pre-defined forms followed by plant life throughout its development.

The piece starts from a purely geometric basis, as the designer first creates an ellipse, to which he adds layer upon layer of honeycomb cardboard, gradually contorting the shape to create a "flow" of material, with its own individual tensions and cadences, allowing the user to recline.

Che Eyzenbach's Start It Up range is an economical solution to the problems of finding affordable furniture encountered by students or young couples. Start it up comprises a wardrobe, table, and two chairs, constructed from recyclable honeycomb cardboard, that customers assemble themselves and integrated packaging that converts into coat hangers and a table lamp, minimising waste.

opposite
Flow 1
2009.
Honeycomb cardboard.
75 x 75 x 40 cm.

top and bottom
Flow 3
2009.
Honeycomb cardboard.
160 x 80 x 65 cm.
All images courtesy
Che Eyzenbach.

Flexible Love™

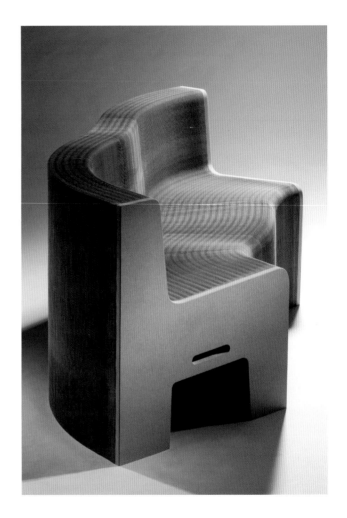

Manufactured by Taiwanese company Pinzaan, Flexible Love™ is a modular, extendable sofa, inspired by the traditional two-berth loveseat. Constructed using an "accordion-like" honeycomb cardboard structure to create durable seating, Flexible Love™ is made from fully recycled paper wood waste materials, and is produced using pre-existing manufacturing processes in order to minimise harm to the environment.

The idea of Flexible Love™ was conceived by Taiwanese designer Chise Chiu, who exercised his flair for design while working at his family's small chain of cardboard and electronics factories. Partly by chance, but also through experimenting with different forms of cardboard, Chiu came up with the idea of using a honeycomb structure to create furniture with unusual flexible qualities. After locating a specialist producer of honeycomb cardboard in Taipei, he further explored the potential of the material, creating rigid cardboard seating platforms by extending the compressed, concertinaed cardboard.

above, opposite and
overleaf
Flexible Love™ ECO 8
2009.
Recycled cardboard
folded dimensions:
64 x 56 x 13 cm,
stretched dimensions:
64 x 56 x 350 cm.
Courtesy Flexible Love.™

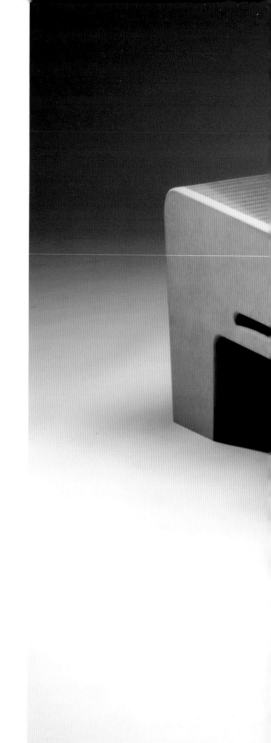

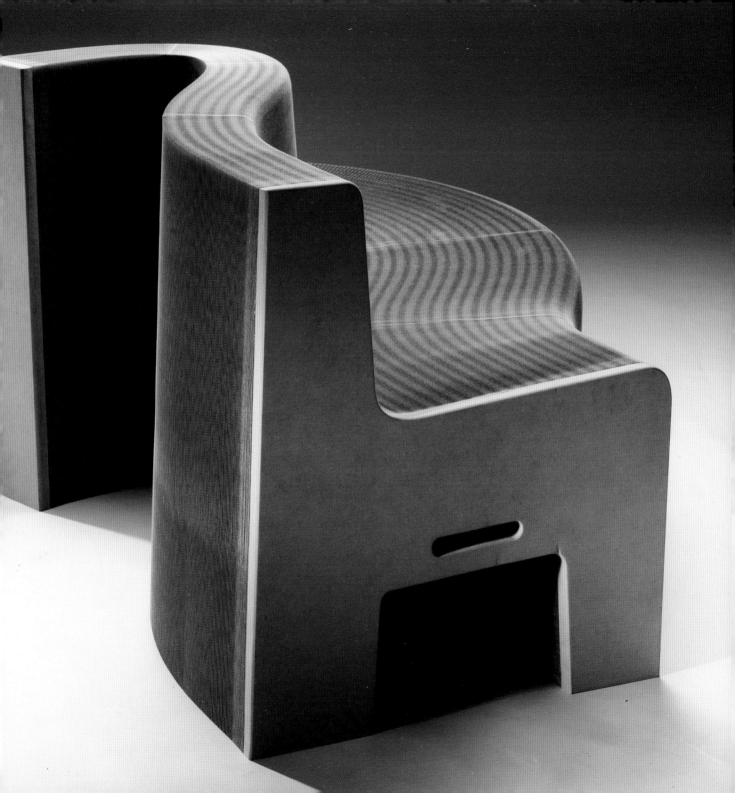

Frank Gehry

Frank Gehry's iconic Wiggle Chair is one of various cardboard furniture creations designed by the Canadian-American architect Frank Gehry, otherwise known for the architectural design of the Guggenheim Bilbao. Gehry's fascination with the manipulation of basic, utilitarian materials led to his experimentation with the material. Using a process whereby he layered sheets of corrugated cardboard, Gehry was able to bend and shape the resulting structure to form various shapes of exponential strength, which were then finished with a sheet of hardboard to further enhance durability.

The Easy Edges line of furniture, 1969–1972—from which the Wiggle Chair was borne—combines sleek, subtle design, with Gehry's expert engineering knowledge that saw the material take on a whole new design aesthetic. Other items in the series include the Side Chair, Dining Table and Low Table Set, all of which are still available today from the furniture store Vitra.

Gehry's increasing interest in the possibilities of cardboard design materialised in his second line of furniture: the Experimental Edges series, 1983. Combining sheets of cardboard of varying widths, Gehry produced these items of furniture, sculptural in style that exhibited the architect's critical eye for detail and meticulous craftsmanship.

above
Low Table
1971.
Corrugated cardboard.
39 x 43 x 39 cm.

opposite
Wiggle Chair
1971.
Corrugated cardboard.
Copyright Vitra,
www.vitra.com.

David Graas

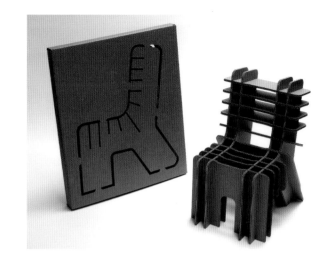

Cardboard has a special resonance for David Graas. It is evocative of the incidental, overlooked, everyday materials that sparked his interest in design, and with which he created his first works of art as a young child.

It was through use of reclaimed materials that Graas articulated his artistic credo: that good design requires less, not more, detail; that stripping away unnecessary detail was a way of improving an object's quality; and that by transforming ostensibly worthless materials into objects perceived as valuable was the optimal way of making his own distinctive imprint on design.

Graas' pieces are intentionally interactive, a theme in keeping with his belief in the universality of furniture. For example, his 2007 Dutch Design Award nominated Finish It Yourself, a children's furniture series that combines packaging, product and assembly instructions within a single piece of recyclable corrugated cardboard. Integrative packaging is featured across the entire Graas range—in Not a Lamp, 2004, as well as FIY (Finish It Yourself), 2004 and 2007's Don't spill your dinner table line. Cardboard Lounge, 2009, utilised computer-guided cutting processes to form each interlocking component part, flat-packed, and ready for assembly by the customer. The result is a visually stunning piece, with precision-cut contouring that provides comfort in lieu of upholstery.

opposite
Don't spill your coffee table
2007.
Corrugated cardboard.
72 x 72 x 43 cm.

top
FIY (Finish It Yourself) Junior
2007.
Corrugated cardboard.
30 x 44 x 48 cm.

bottom
Cardboard Lounge
2009.
Corrugated cardboard.
80 x 80 x 74 cm.

Habitat

This folded chair—created by David Wilson for the upmarket lifestyle store Habitat—is diminutive in size, but incredibly sturdy due to its origami-inspired star design and use of heavy corrugated cardboard as a building material. Though produced as furniture for children, the chair's retro minimal appearance—and surprising comfort—would doubtless appeal to the more discerningly design-conscious adult.

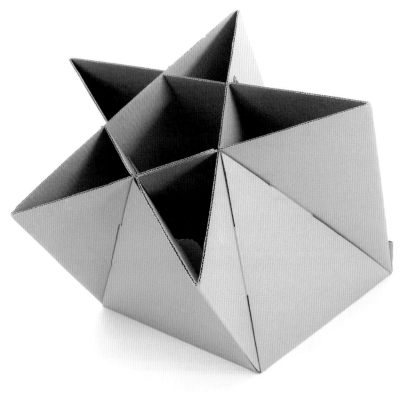

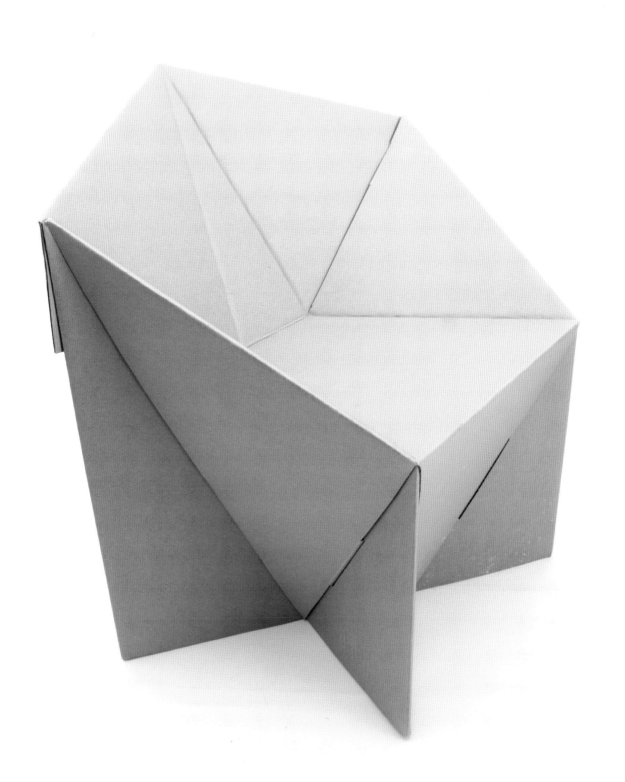

Alex Hellum

Alex Hellum's work in cardboard encapsulates his philosophy of design, producing organic, authentic and functional pieces with a natural longevity through the use of reclaimed and vernacular materials.

While the genesis of his ideas comes from a pragmatic resolve to provide practicality in design, his pieces possess a whimsical, playful charm, borne out in their clean lines and gentle contours—a quality which translates visibly into his furniture for children. There is a boldness and spirit of individuality in each of his cardboard designs, which reflects Hellum's independent outlook: he produces furniture in low volumes, allowing him the creative freedom to control every precise detail of the design process.

Born in Larvik, Norway in 1966, Hellum first trained at The Buckinghamshire Chilterns University College between 1992 and 1994, before going on to study Furniture Design at the Royal College of Art, graduating in 1996.

Following his graduation, Hellum received a grant from the Craft Council to establish his own design practice and subsequently has worked on numerous private and commercial design commissions, creating products for London furniture boutique Heals, UK-based distributor Thorsten Van Elten and British design company Ercol. The bulk of his output, however, is sold directly to interior designers and the general public.

above
Papp 1 Chair
2009.
270 x 350 x 350 cm.

opposite
Papp 2 Horse
2009.
380 x 130 x 380 cm.

It Design

Swiss company It Design—formed by architects Valérie Jomini and Stanislas Zimmermann—have been making modern urban furniture since 1997, prizing themselves on "making compact and flexible furniture for young and mobile urbanites".

The Itbed—futon and mattress—is a seven millimetre-thick corrugated cardboard sheet, measuring 25 cm high and between 90 and 160 cm wide. The Itbed futon can be used to support either futon or thinner roll-up mattresses, its concertinaed profile being supported from head to foot by two lengths of webbing, rendering it robust enough to carry the weight of a mattress and several persons. Its structure also means that it can be easily collapsed into a portable bundle, making it ideal accommodation for guests and frequent movers.

The Itbed mattress, on the other hand, has been made for use with more traditional mattresses—the cardboard rests underneath—making it suitable for everyday use.

above and opposite
Itbed futon + mattress
Corrugated cardboard.
200 cm x variable widths.

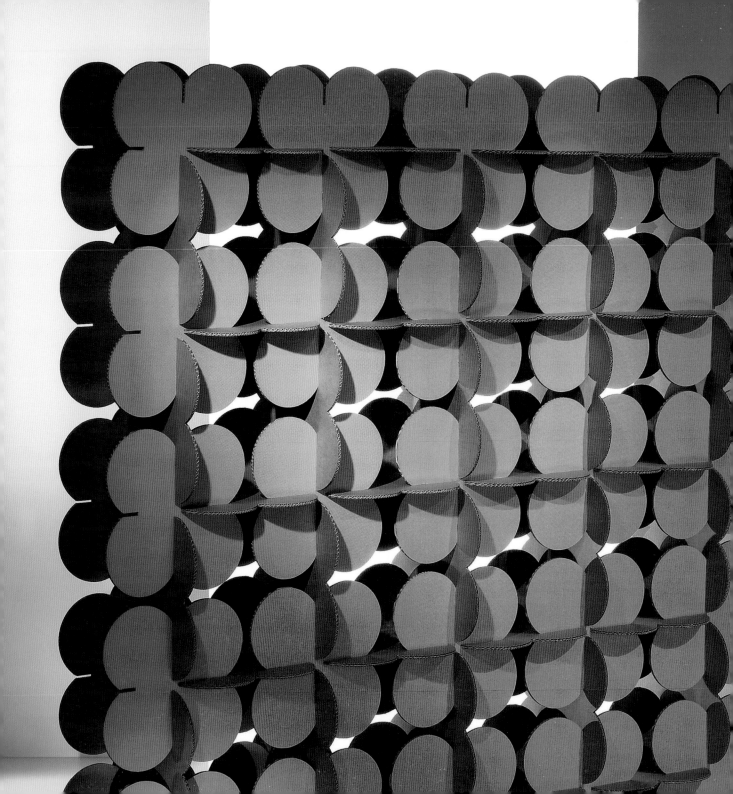

Kube Design

Italian design house Kube employ compressed, corrugated and stratified cardboard as a structural, as well as a cosmetic, material to create pieces that evoke both modern and postmodern styles, marrying it with more conventional materials to create striking textural and visual effects.

Cardboard's versatility is reflected by its prominence in modular pieces, such as Fiorello, a coated nylon floral pattern partition; and Jack, an adaptable table and magazine rack. Coarse corrugated cardboard is juxtaposed against smooth acrylic surfaces, creating playful and irreverent pieces: the crunching angles of Rock, the dreamy, whimsical curves of Sgas and Tatoo's mock ornamental table legs. Cardboard lends the pieces accessibility and liveliness, enhanced by vibrant colour schemes.

opposite
Fiorello
Corrugated/stratified
cardboard.
100 x 100 x 32 cm.

top left
Tatoo
150 x 74 x 75 cm.

top right
Tatoo Baby
75 x 74 x 75 cm.

bottom
Mesa (**large**)
Corrugated/stratified
cardboard.
150 x 74 x 75cm.
All images courtesy
Kube Design.

Lazerian and Richard Sweeney

Furniture designer Liam Hopkins and artist Richard Sweeney's collaborative Honeycomb range of furniture explores the technical possibilities of cardboard—here shown in the Bravais Armchair and Radiolarian Sofa. Using locally sourced corrugated cardboard, Hopkins and Sweeney's designs were inspired by structural forms recurring throughout nature: for example the shape of a wasp's nest, or the crystalline bone structures of microscopic sea organisms known as 'Radiolaria', hence the name of the Honeycomb sofa.

From this initial interest, Hopkins and Sweeney began to experiment with various shapes and forms, generating images using computer-aided design. The composition of these visuals, primarily consisted of triangular columns that mimicked the conical forms taken as initial inspiration for their work—a configuration that purposefully utilised the structural properties of cardboard.

From this, each individual component for the pieces was created using flat layouts taken from the virtual model, and used to create templates, from which each constituent cardboard part was created. These parts were then cut by hand and glued together to form the Bravais Armchair and Radiolarian Sofa, the latter of which was made up of over 2000 different parts.

Bravais Armchair
2010.
Corrugated cardboard.

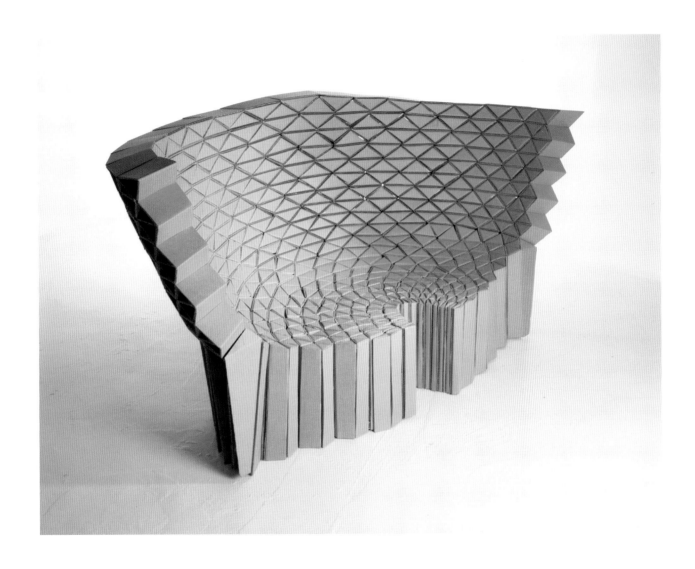

above and overleaf
Radiolarian Sofa
2010.
Corrugated cardboard.

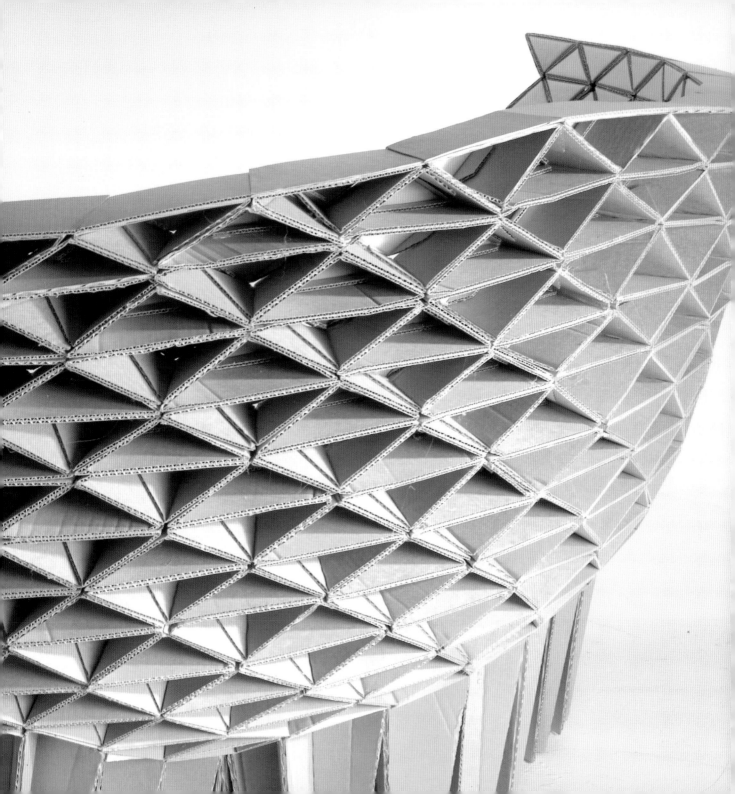

Paper Tiger

From its humble beginnings utilising cardboard waste, Paper Tiger—founded by Australian designer Anthony Dann as an idea to subsidise his architectural studies—has gained international recognition for the company's cardboard stools.

Made from up to 70 per cent recycled content, with the remaining virgin pulp being taken from salvaged timber scrap, the stools also boast being 100 per cent recyclable. The product has even gained the title of "Ecospecifier" by the Australian Environmental Certification Company, produced with local manufacturing in mind.

The furniture's graphic identity is also a key consideration of Dann's—viewing cardboard's surface as a blank canvas, onto which designs can be created; a particularly favourable aspect considering its marketing as an item of children's furniture. The material also provides a safe surface with which children can play, as well as meaning it can be easily recycled once they grow out of it.

right
Paper Tiger Feedaway
Recycled cardboard.

opposite
Paper Tiger Stool
2006.
Recycled cardboard.
60 x 53 x 45 cm.

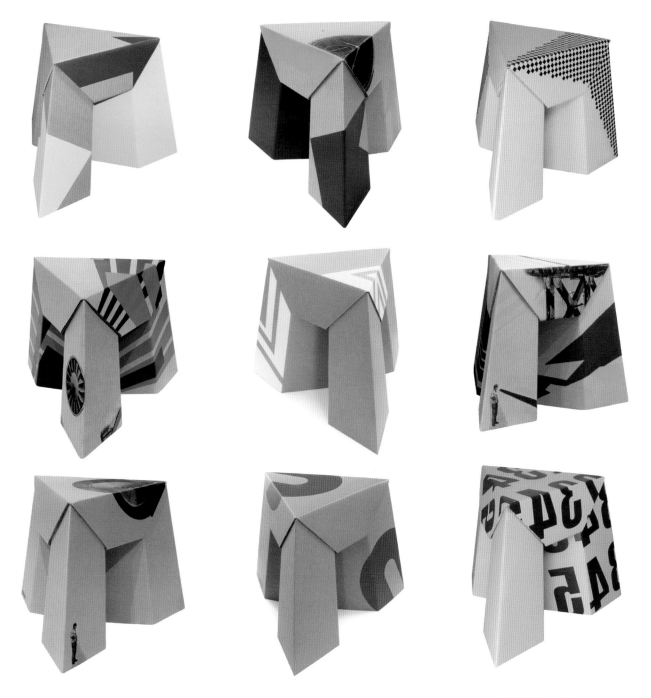

Raacke Design

Peter Raacke's Otto series, first made available for sale in 1968, has proven a seminal work in cardboard furniture design. Raacke was the first major designer to conceive of cardboard as a viable material for furniture and marketed the Otto series as an inexpensive, highly customisable alternative to furniture made from conventional woods and metals.

Raacke's cardboard designs have a perceptibly modern, industrial aesthetic, with the theme of mass-production and accessibility running heavily throughout his work. Nevertheless, his cardboard creations, like his Mono series of cutlery, retain a compelling individuality that has seen the Museum of Modern Art in San Francisco and the Guggenheim Museum in Bilbao recognise their influence in exhibitions of influential design.

Now enjoying extensive reproduction in Europe, Otto is made from pieces of interlocking corrugated cardboard and in its original range comprised storage units and tables as well as seating. Raacke is pioneering for more than just his use of materials, as he first approached the concept of sustainability in furniture design long before global interest in environmental preservation became vogue.

His company, Raacke Design, was founded in 1958 and is his vehicle for commercial collaborations with firms across the world. Born in 1928, Raacke was educated at the Drawing Academy, Hanau and the École Nationale Supérieure des Beaux-Arts, Paris. He retired in 1994.

Otto
1968.

Real-Made

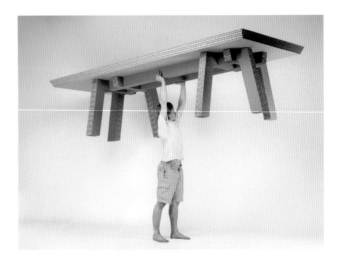

Arno Mathies and Fabien Capéran set-up Real-Made after studying Industrial Design together at École Cantonale d'Art de Lausanne, Switzerland. Their focus was to create durable products using innovative techniques that explore new possibilities within the field of product design.

The Gruff set is a range of mountable and dismountable cardboard furniture using 1.5 cm and 0.7 cm planks of layered cardboard, that are assembled using housing joints. A separate cardboard or glass tabletop—depending on which version the customer chooses; there is also a printed cardboard version available—is placed upon legs to provide stability for the table and, similarly, cardboard planks are placed upon cardboard feet for the shelving units. According to Mathies and Capéran, "Gruff is a response to the paradox of a society focused on increasing consumption while trying to achieve sustainable development".

By giving the customer a choice of combination of materials—cardboard, printed cardboard, glass—within their products, it is thought they are giving them greater control over the sustainability of the items they purchase—allowing them to choose between a disposable or permanent piece of furniture.

opposite bottom
Gruff Bench
Corrugated cardboard
and glass.
125 x 49 x 43 cm

above and opposite top
Gruff Tables
Corrugated cardboard
and glass.
105 x 75 x 255 cm

opposite right
Gruff Shelving
Corrugated cardboard
and glass.
220 x 92 x 200 cm

All images courtesy
of Arno Mathies of
Real-Made.
Photos Florian Joye
and Michel Bonvin.

Sruli Recht

Sruli Recht's career began in fashion design, from which his interests have expanded to encompass industrial and furniture design. Recht's design process gives precedence to the creative process, often dictating the finer details of the finished "non-product", without determining its wider appearance in "the blend of organic geometry".

2008's Cutting Table No. 1 emanated in concept from Recht's itinerant lifestyle and the complaints of designs students lacking a compact, ergonomic surface on which to work. Cutting Table No. 1 is light, sturdy, fully collapsible and made from recyclable corrugated cardboard, complete with a carrying case, three drawers and a laminated surface that meets the requirements of the travelling designer and the student for whom space is a luxury.

Recht's work over the last eight years has included creating costume for film and video installations; numerous private commissions; pattern cutting and showpiece construction for the late British fashion designer Alexander McQueen; exclusive research and development for high tech fabric developers; and a role as head designer and consultant for a number of fashion labels in Iceland and Australia. His products, garments and artwork have been exhibited through Asia, Australia, Scandinavia, Russia, the Americas and Europe.

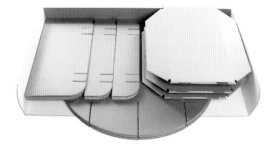

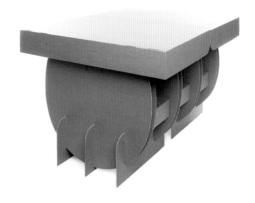

Cutting Table No. 1
2008.
150 x 120 x 93 cm.
Courtesy Sruli Recht.

Hans Sandgren Jakobsen

Born in Copenhagen in 1963, Hans Sandgren Jakobsen was originally trained as a cabinet maker. He proceeded to study industrial design at The Danish Design School in Copenhagen, after which he spent time in America observing the carpentry techniques of protestant Shaker communities, renowned for their simple, functional and high-quality furniture. Since graduating, he has also worked in Japan, where he observed Far Eastern design techniques.

In 1997 Jokobsen established his own design practice in Greena, Denmark, where he has worked for a number of high profile clients. Marrying functionality with minimalist form, Jakobsen's attention to detail is paramount to his work, with each item following a lengthy design process from sketch to final product. His vast portfolio includes numerous items including chairs, tables, furnishings and children's furniture.

Jakobsen's Viper screenwall, is a synthesis of these many styles: highly functional and modern in design, yet elegant and visually self-serving. Made from a number of connecting paper tubes, filled with sound absorbent foam, the Viper is a modular and highly flexible partition, whose vertical ellipses fluidly adapt to different spaces. The rich texture of the cardboard and its organic build is conducive to Jakobsen's personal design ethic: "The material cardboard is very honest and environmentally compatible, and therefore I find it very suitable to work with."

Viper screenwall
1996.
Paper tubes.
160 x 300 cm.
Courtesy Hans
Sandgren Jakobsen.

Riki Watanabe/ Metrocs

Originally designed by Riki Watanabe in 1965—one of the pioneers of post-war Japanese design—and reproduced since 2006 by Metrocs—an "interior design brand line" that specialises in European and Japanese product design—the Carton Furniture Series shows how simple, inexpensive design can simultaneously be original and innovative, as celebrated in Watanabe's winning of the Mainichi Industrial Design Prize for the Kid's Set in 1967.

The Carton Furniture series includes a Kids Set, High Stool and Low Stool, all of which are made without using any adhesives; each item is constructed entirely from cleverly folded recycled cardboard, which the customer assembles themselves at home. The result is a surprisingly sturdy product—Watanabe seeing the potential strength in paper based materials, influenced by the Japanese origami culture.

The range also comes in a variety of different colour co-ordinations, hence its appeal as a both a design item and a piece of children's furniture.

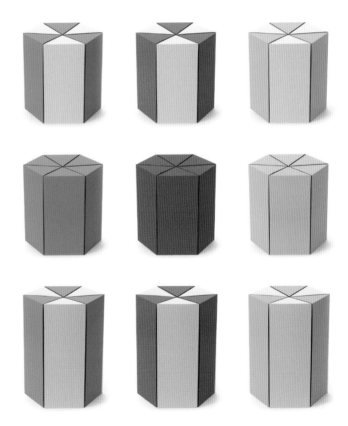

top and centre
Carton Furniture
Series Stool (Low)
1965/2006.
33 x 33 x 33 cm.

bottom
Carton Furniture
Series Stool (High)
1965/2006.
33 x 33 x 42 cm.

Carton Furniture
Series Kid's Set Stool
1965/2006.
22 x 22 x 22 cm.

Carton Furniture
Series Kid's Set Table
1965/2006.
44 x 44 x 33 cm.
All images courtesy
Metrocs.

WEmake

WEmake Tetris is part of the design company's 'WEmake Inspirations' that "encourage the recipient to produce their own WEmake product". Working from a philosophy to: "make… you smile… you think… you make" WEmake's design inspirations and products are marketed with a sustainable design ethic at their core.

Tetris—"the worlds cheapest designer furniture system", sold for £2 from the company's website—encourages the customer to make their own cardboard furniture, offering a range of possibilities including a dining table, a nest of tables, an easy chair, a magazine rack and a stool.

All of the designs available are based around the same 10 cm grid pattern, from which the user is advised to use scrap cardboard that would otherwise end up in landfill sites, and, following the WEmake instructions, cut and laminate the constituent parts to form their chosen piece of furniture.

Tetris
Waste cardboard.
Sizes variable.

TETRIS **WE**make
inspiration #02

Things you might find useful:
- ☐ Metal Ruler
- ☐ Scissors
- ☐ Pencil
- ☐ Cardboard
- ☐ Glue (PVA)
- ☐ Cutting mat
- ☐ Varnish or Paint
- ☐ Brush

collect and flatten some nice clean corrugated cardboard... mark out the profile of your Tetris design on the cardboard... take care to alternate the orientation of the corrugation to help give the Tetris structure strength... cut out your shapes with a sharp blade or scissors... glue and stick the Tetris pieces together... place under weight or clamp while drying... when the glue is set protect with varnish or paint if desired... enjoy

waste cardboard piles up on our streets and in our dustbins... add a bit of WEmake Tetris inspiration to make a dining chair... a bed... a nest of tables... an easy chair... a magazine rack... a stool... happy making!

WEmake

Tetris 00 1:1

This is meant as inspiration for qualified persons only. You should satisfy yourself as to the suitability of your materials, the appropriateness of your tools and the structural integrity of your constructions. Wrong assembly could lead to personal injury or damage... Take care now!

www.**WE**make.co.uk

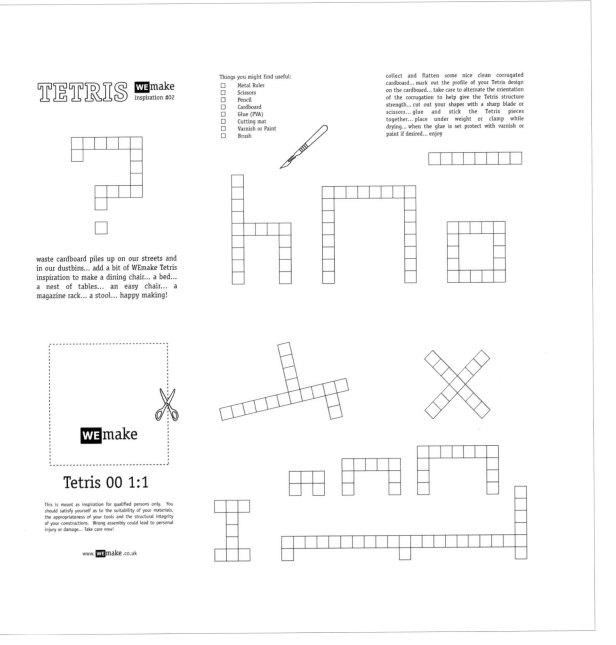

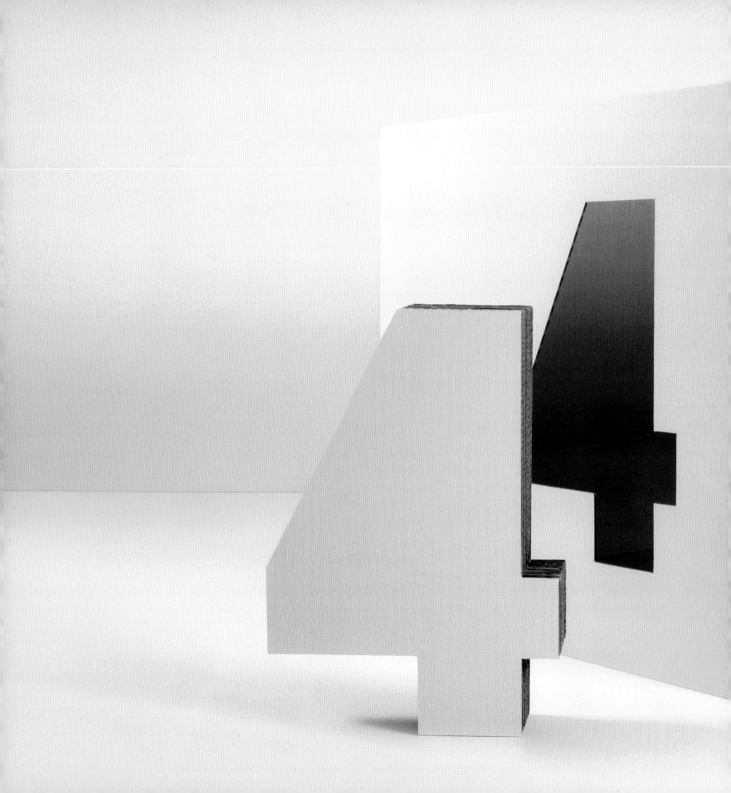

Art and
Architecture

■ Cardboard has been used in art for many years, as a cheap canvas or as a material with which to create collages or sculptures. Picasso favoured the material, as seen in his sculpture *Guitar*, 1912, as did Robert Rauschenberg with his *Cardboard and Related Pieces* series. This trend is continued in the following chapter, as it profiles a number of artists who use cardboard as a medium, from Thomas Demand's full-scale three-dimensional models, to Tobias Putrih's installations that explore ideas of fragility and precariousness.

On the other hand, architecture's cardboard heritage remains much more recent; its prevalence increasing with the continual blurring of boundaries between art and architecture, as seen in the various installations shown throughout the chapter—from Fantastic Norway Architect's *Cardboard Cloud* to CJ Lim/Studio 8 Architect's *Seasons through the Looking Glass*.

Alongside these, cardboard has increasingly been used as a material with which architects have been navigating interior and exterior architectures; its distinct functional use, in this context, providing an experimental aspect to their work. From *Cardboard Café*, as seen in interior design firm B3's contribution to the 2009 London Design Week, to the *Mafoombey* listening booth—a space designed to listen to music within; and of course, Shigeru Ban's impressive career through which he has expressed a continued devotion to the use of cardboard and paper in creating various different structures internationally, their ephemeral beauty once again reminding the reader of the close relationship between art and architecture.

B3 Designers

If the accelerated increase in the number of pop-up shops, bars and café is characteristic of a hype-driven culture, with a short attention span, the *Cardboard Café*—created by interior design firm B3 for the London Design Festival—pays testament to this statement with its week-long, terminable structure. Built out of 8000 boxes, the sides of which were coloured in a distinctive fluorescent orange colour, the construction of the café was then assembled within B3's studio, with two large cardboard archways flanking the entrance onto the street outside.

A fully functioning space, serving coffee during the day and cocktails in the evening, the *Cardboard Café* lived up to its name with its interior made entirely from the titular material—from the tables and chairs right down to the cups. Inside, the contours of the bar walls were spotlit to augment the overall textural effect. Like the cursory, interiors-focused hotspots that it mimics, the *Cardboard Café* does not endure, but was not built to do so—testified by the fact that it was partially destroyed by a vehicle which was later driven through the archways. Subsequently either recycled or given to students at Goldsmiths University brick-by-brick, the *Cardboard Café* mirrored the whims of a fickle crowd by being a venue that was proudly—and quite literally—disposable.

Cardboard Café
2009.
Courtesy B3 Designers.

Shigeru Ban

Japanese architect Shigeru Ban has earned international acclaim for his paper-tube structures, intended for both temporary and permanent use. Impressed by cardboard's durability and strength, Ban came to refer to cardboard as "improved wood"—an idea that eventually lead to his development of emergency paper tube structures. These architectures, intended to aid natural disaster victims in poverty stricken countries, were first initiated after the Kobe earthquake, where Ban used 34-ply tubes to build a community hall and houses; he has since created 'disaster relief projects' for the victims of the Niigata earthquake, Japan in 2004; the Sri Lankan tsunami in 2007; and the Sichuan earthquake in 2008.

Made from recycled cardboard, the paper tubes with which Ban creates his structures have been used on projects as varied as the Miyake Design Studio Gallery, Tokyo in 1994, based upon the Grecian agora, where by a space is created using columns—in this case paper tube columns— and shade; the *Japan Pavilion* at the Expo 2000, Hannover— a huge arched paper-tube structure based upon a brief of producing as little industrial waste as possible when dismantled; and the *Vasarely Pavilion*, Aix-en-Provence, France, in 2006—a homage to the artist Paul Cézanne, for the Cézanne in Province festival. Alongside these projects Ban has become recognised for numerous other works that include schools, churches, houses and bridges.

above

Vasareley Pavillion
Aix-en-Provence, France,
2006.
Paper tubes.

opposite

*Miyake Design
Studio Gallery*
Shibuya, Tokyo, Japan,
1994.
Paper tubes.

overleaf

Japan Pavillion
2000.
Paper tubing.
All images courtesy
Shigeru Ban Architects.

Kyle Bean

Graphic designer Kyle Bean recreates iconic pieces of modern technology—a camera, iPod and mobile phone, amongst others—as products entirely made from recycled corrugated cardboard, each of which has been inserted with a small battery pack, overlaid with tracing paper to create a glowing 'screen'. The premise for this particular project is based around the notion of disposability. If cardboard is supposedly a material that swiftly becomes redundant once its original purpose has been fulfilled, then Bean's work indicates that the fate of consumer technology is fundamentally no different. Momentarily desirable, then succeeded by better, newer models and made instantly obsolete and unfashionable, the trend towards continually 'upgrading' is acknowledged as an equally wasteful process. The suggestion is qualified by the material itself—already widely accepted as replaceable and cheap, the cardboard might be masquerading as a high-value object, but the fact that it is invites us to question the value of what we term as disposable.

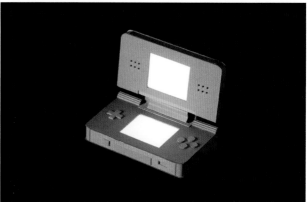

Disposable Technology
Variable sizes.
Courtesy Kyle Bean.

Paul Coudamy

Parisian designer Paul Coudamy was commissioned—and challenged—by advertising agency Beast to build an office in a single month in a 180 m² industrial space, on a limited budget. It was additionally expected to provide workspace for 20 people along with storage and meeting rooms with acoustic insulation for privacy. Providing a solution that accounted for both practical and financial restrictions, the result was a room constructed from 4 cm thick water-resistant honeycomb cardboard put together with tape and wood glue. Generally conceding to the material's functional possibilities, the design was made up of separate, movable units meaning it could be rearranged as necessary, while the meeting room was reinterpreted as a cardboard pod. The space comprised of 20 work stations, separated by dividing walls which also function as tables and shelving units and feature beach-chair like seats. Proving a unique take on the standardised experience of office life, the design also featured lampshades made from umbrellas.

Beast office
2008.
Honeycomb cardboard.
Courtesy Paul Coudamy.

Thomas Demand

In the first instance, Thomas Demand's large-scale photographic works confront viewers with scenes of a sober simplicity, largely unremarkable but for the precise and lucid manner with which they have been captured. Upon closer inspection, however, an uncanny sense of artifice begins to dominate; everyday objects exhibit unfamiliar qualities, there is an absence of details we expect to see and our confidence in what we recognise becomes undermined.

Demand's photographs in fact present full-scale three-dimensional models, skilfully and meticulously assembled from cardboard and coloured paper, which reconstruct scenes from pre-existing mass media photographs. These scenes are typically chosen by Demand for their historical, cultural or political significance; his concern is with the veracity of the photographic record and the ways in which mass media images foster mythologies that structure our knowledge and understanding of the world. As such, within Demand's practice, the basic materials of cardboard and coloured paper become endowed with a critical function: textures, forms, light and shade are all rendered with an impressive measure of realism that however retains the qualities of the materials used, allowing for the gradual emergence of subtle but critical imperfections that cause us to reconsider the information we are receiving.

opposite
Fotoecke/Photobooth
2009.
C-Print/Diasec.
180 x 198 cm.
Copyright Thomas Demand. VG Bild-Kunst, Bonn/ DACS, London.

overleaf
Heldenorgel
2009.
C-Print/Diasec.
240 x 380 cm.
Copyright Thomas Demand. VG Bild-Kunst, Bonn/ DACS, London.

Fantastic Norway

Resembling a large pixelated cloud, Fantastic Norway Architects' *Cardboard Cloud* installation, seen here hanging effortlessly from the ceiling of Oslo's Centre for Design and Architecture was used as platform from which Norwegian design students could display their work.

Sweeping across the hall—creating beneath it different shapes and spaces, some of which were filled with objects such as sofas and bikes, others of which were left empty— the *Cardboard Cloud* highlights, on the one hand, and glorifies, on the other, the rudimentary use of the cardboard box.

The thrill of unpacking is fundamental to the concept at the root of Fantastic Norway's *Cardboard Cloud*. Displaying the objects in various states of 'undress', some remained in their boxes, whilst others were on full display.

right, opposite
and overleaf
Cardboard Cloud
2009.
Courtesy Fantastic
Norway Architects.

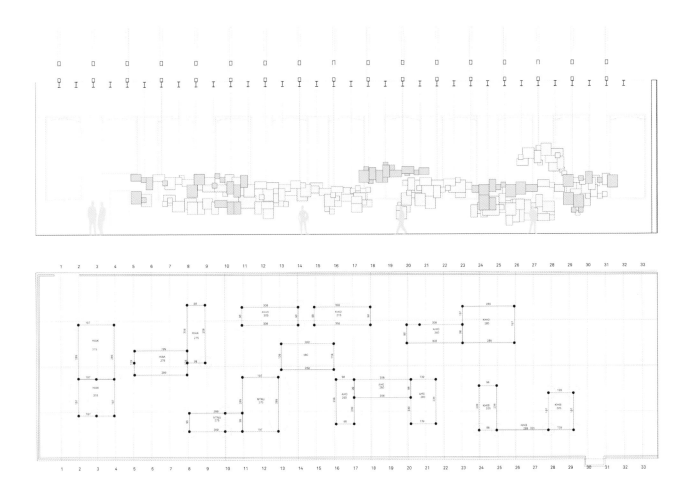

ART AND ARCHITECTURE · 171

Chris Gilmore

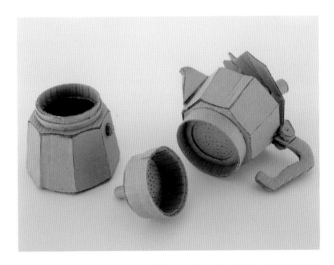

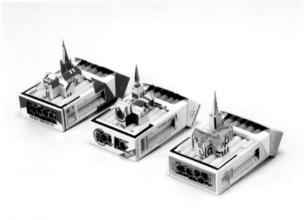

Often recreating objects in painstakingly realistic detail—to the point where viewers believed that the subjects themselves had simply been covered in cardboard—Chris Gilmour's life-size sculptures present us with commonplace objects constructed from plain cardboard packaging and glue. Gilmour's meticulous reproductions of complex mechanical structures—such as bikes, classic cars and typewriters—reveal a fascination with original craftsmanship, with a peculiar dialogue created by such objects of value replicated in a discarded material that is ostensibly of no value. Cardboard, a utilitarian and mass-produced material only ever intended to contain something, is reincarnated as something in its own right—its capacity as a discarded material has been renewed, but paradoxically, it does not function like the thing it represents, and thus material and subject rely on one another for meaning. It is the ritualistic activities of modern consumer life that Gilmour concerns himself with, drawing attention to the values that we attach to material things when copies can be so realistically constructed from that which we throw away. More recently, Gilmour has used branded packaging material to exploit our associations with them, including cigarette packets, which he has built tiny churches from—the religious borne from the ethically irresponsible.

opposite
Fiat 500
2002–2004.
Cardboard and glue.

top
Moka
2002.
Cardboard and glue.

bottom
Churches
2004.
Cigarette boxes and glue.
All images courtesy the artist,
Perugi Artecontemporanea.
Photo Marco De Palma.

Kalliala, Ruskeepää and Lukasczyk

Originally conceived as an entry to a competition devised by Helsinki University, which invited participants to design a small space in which to listen to music, the *Mafoombey* listening booth was an experiment, which proved to be both cheap and acoustically viable. Inspired by the primitive spatiality of caves, the designers initially attempted to use other recycled materials such as carpets. The space itself was imagined as a cube, and was decreed within the rules of the competition to be no more than 2.5 cubic metres squared; it eventually consisted of doubled up pieces of 7 mm thick corrugated cardboard in 360 layers, that were internally supported by cardboard columns running through the structure. Lights and speakers were incorporated into the layers and emitted into the hollow space within, which featured seating, a CD player, and surround sound—essentially a modern, luxury experience at negligible cost. The interior was initially modelled in clay, its contours recreated on the team's computer, before the Finnish paper manufacturers Stora Enso provided them with a program to manufacture the sliced horizontal stack. *Mafoombey* was later shortlisted for the Design Forum prize for best Nordic Building and exhibited at Helsinki's Lahti University of Applied Sciences.

opposite
Mafoombey
2005.
Corrugated cardboard.
250 x 250 x 250 cm.

overleaf
Mafoombey (interior)
All images courtesy
Kalliala, Ruskeepää
and Lukasczyk.

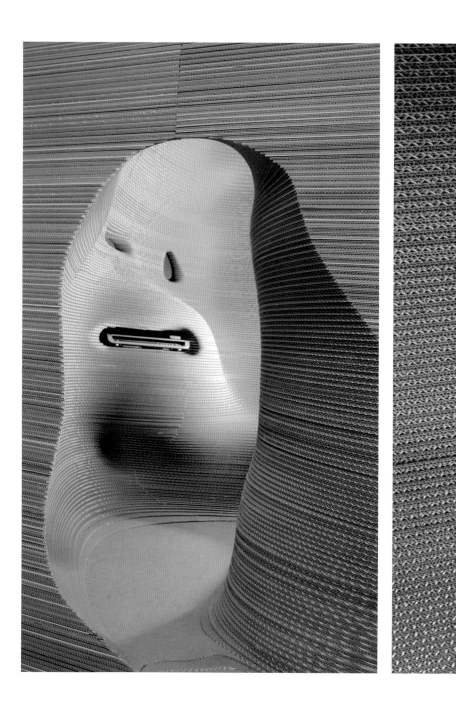

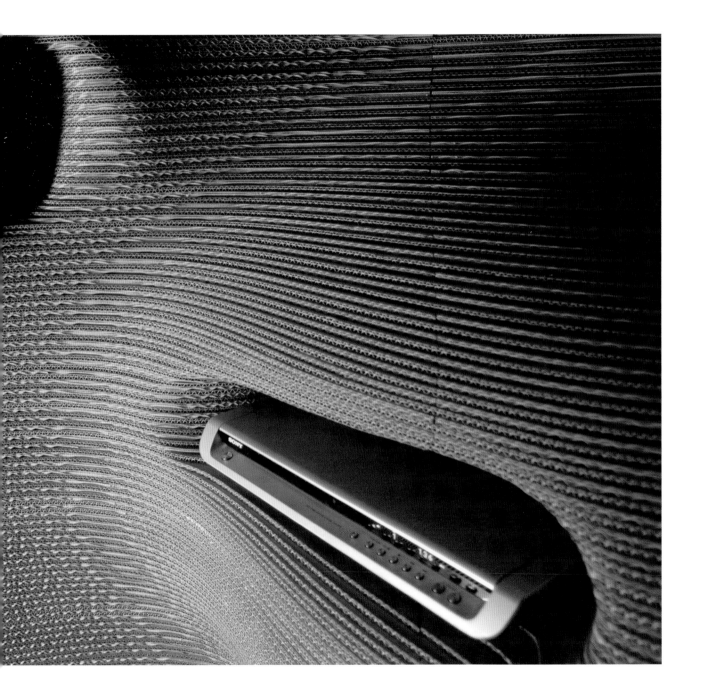

Karis

Assenting to an increasingly competitive market in which fashion brands are presenting their lines to consumers in innovative environments, boutique Karis— located in a Hiroshima shopping centre—had Japanese architectural firm Suppose Design Office re-imagine their shop interior with different lengths of clustered cardboard tubes. Aiming to provide a memorable shopping experience, the jutting, sloping ceilings were constructed to resemble the conditions of caves, where the light, atmosphere or view of the space would alter depending on where one stands. From certain perspectives full views of the shop are on offer, while from others customers find themselves contained within inner partitions. While being entirely artificial, particularly in its use of a recycled product, its mimicking of an organic environment with a complex and ostensibly random structure meant shopping within it could be perceived as a simulation of a walk through nature. Through the transformation of the space it is hoped that customers will look at products differently—indicating that cardboard can just as well be reused in a commercially savvy way.

Karis shop interior
2010.
Paper tubes.
Courtesy Karis and
Suppose Design Office.

Le Gun

To launch the fourth issue of their illustration-led magazine, East London-based art collective Le Gun as part of their *The Family* exhibition constructed a sitting room entirely made from cardboard in the Rochelle School in Shoreditch. Open to the public for a week, and funded by arts commissioning body NOMAD and A-Foundation, the work comprised pen and ink detailed 1930's style furnishings including floorboards, paintings, light fittings and carpets. Visitors were invited to step through a small, Alice in Wonderland inspired door that led into the cardboard space. The seating, including armchairs, a sofa and a piano stool, were fully functioning, inked in Le Gun's characteristically surrealist style. In the corner of the room was a mini-grand piano richly illustrated with a flapper-style woman swathed in demonic-looking monsters, while the bookshelf included titles such as *Classic Chess Moves in Russia and China* and *My Life in Cake*.

The Family
2008.
Cardboard, pen and ink.
Photos Michele Panzeri.

CJ Lim/ Studio 8 Architects

CJ Lim/Studio 8 Architects' installation at the Victoria and Albert Museum, London that ran for a year from March 2008 to March 2009, was loosely based upon Lewis Carroll's novel *Alice's Adventures in Wonderland* and the notion of "mythical underground spaces".

Created inside the tunnel entrance of the museum, *Seasons through the Looking Glass* explores the "spatial possibilities of a subterranean garden" by creating an abstract structure from honeycomb cardboard, representing the intertwined trunks and branches of an underground garden. Within these branches "roses" were inserted, made from recycled fabric samples; these were subtly altered over the course of the installation's lifespan to reflect the changing seasons.

CJ Lim/Studio 8 Architects are a multi-disciplinary architectural practice with a focus on cultural, social and environmental sustainability.

Seasons through the Looking Glass 2008–2009. Honeycomb cardboard and recycled fabric samples. Courtesy CJ Lim/ Studio 8 Architects.

Magma

With the entire interior constructed of treated cardboard—including shelving, changing rooms and counter surfaces—and predominately arriving flat packed, much of the Magma Art Bookshop was unfolded and put together on its Covent Garden site; although the makers did, however, admit that the planning stages of the project had been "vastly laborious and time consuming". The fact that parts could be readily and separately assembled meant that units could be in a constant cycle of use and replacement, and subsequently was both easy and inexpensive to maintain—depending on "how many coffee cups are spilled on them", and attesting to the idea that while vulnerability was a factor, it could be straightforwardly accounted for. Squares behind the shelving system, used to display books and magazines, were backlit exacerbating its honeycomb-like appearance. The back area of the shop functioned as a grotto-like display area, conceding to more textural elements, including hand-cut laminated and gradated cardboard. Other necessary features of the shop were fully functioning: the main shop counter comprised display units, a cash register and storage, as well as its strong surface, and the changing rooms were constructed from panels of cardboard tubes which slid across one another to close.

Magma shop interior
2007.
Courtesy Magma.

Nothing

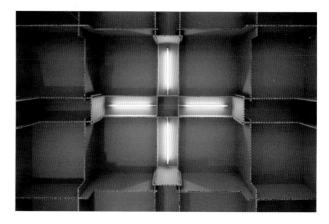

Taking their name from the concept that you can create 'something' from nothing, Amsterdam-based commercial, creative agency Nothing physicalised the premise by using cardboard—a material we regard to be of no use—to help build an office, ostensibly a symbol of functioning, day-to-day life. Making up much of the interior, the walls, beams, shelving and a set of stairs are made from 500 square metres of reinforced cardboard, and uniquely were treated as a blank canvas for visitors to draw or write on, and include the work of illustrator Fiodor Sumkin. Meant as material translation of a more existential comment on the power of ideas, Nothing aimed to make their consumers part of their brand by engaging them in a experience which required a form of creative participation. No glue or other form of fixing was used, and the 1500 pieces instead slotted together meaning it could be easily disassembled.

Nothing office interior
2009.
Courtesy Nothing and
Joost Van Bleiswijk.

O-S Architects

Creating an even grander entrance than usual to the Hotel Saint-Côme, Paris, O-S Architects' temporary installation for the Festival des Architectures Vives 2008, challenges the staid and uninspiring stereotype often associated with cardboard.

The geometric corridor, constructed using 40 x 40 cm cardboard boxes, is lined with a gold reflective material that casts an illuminating glow across the hotel's courtyard, welcoming visitors through. Throughout this corridor, boxes have been removed, to allow the renaissance architecture from outside in, and the juxtaposing gleam of the cardboard installation's interior out.

Back Side Flip 360°
2008.
Cardboard boxes.
40 m².
Courtesy O-S Architects.

Tobias Putrih

The works of Slovenian artist Tobias Putrih range from intuitively constructed, small-scale maquettes, which sketch out ambitious structures that could exist beyond the gallery space; to intricately designed, large-scale architectural installations that dramatically alter the way a space can be experienced. A physics student before pursuing art, his practice is clearly influenced by the logic, discipline and rigour of scientific inquiry. However, despite the complex and dynamic forms Putrih's structures take, they often remain dominated by a sense of deliberate precariousness and fragility, due largely to the artists use of everyday materials such as plywood, packing tape and cardboard.

Underpinning Putrih's practice is an inquiry into the effects that scientific, design and architectural disciplines can have within a social space, together with a desire to relate the fractured and culturally introverted post-war history of the former Yugoslavia to the history and practices of Western Modernism. As such, an interest in cultural institutions and social spaces runs throughout his work, most notably in his various designs for cinema theatres, which attempt to disrupt the passivity of the traditional cinematic experience and encourage viewers to a more conscious engagement with their surroundings.

top
Cardboard cinema at Star City exhibition, Nottingham Contemporary, UK. 2010.
Courtesy Max Protetch.

bottom
Screening Space Related to *What is a Thought Experiment, Anyhow?* 2007–2008.
By Runa Islam. Cardboard, tape, styrofoam, OSB plates, monofilament, metal hooks, fluorescent tubes, lights, colour filters, film projectors, and screens.
800 x 120 x 50 cm.
Courtesy Galleria Civica del Comune di Modena and Max Protetch.
Photo Paolo Terzi.

above
Macula (Series B)
2006.
Dimensions variable.
Courtesy Max Protetch.

overleaf
Argos Cinema
Installation view,
Forms of Resistance,
Van Abbemuseum,
2007.
Plywood and cardboard,
Dimensions variable.
Courtesy Max Protetch.

Sylvie Reno

French artist Sylvie Reno specialises in sculptures made entirely from recycled cardboard. From miniature toothbrushes, to full-scale bank vaults, Reno's work never veers from her material of choice, with each piece including the same attention to detail and intricate finishes. Such accuracy results in Reno's pieces appearing to possess a linear smoothness and serenity, otherwise un-associated with the rigid texture and appearance of cardboard.

right
En route vers la gloire
2003.
Corrugated cardboard.
All images courtesy
the artist.

opposite
La salle des étais
2007.
Corrugated cardboard.

Stealth.
unlimited

Dutch architecture firm Stealth.unlimited "consider space both a tool and an agency, and focus on innovative aspects of sometimes hidden, temporary or unplanned urban practices that challenge ways in which to create physical aspects of the city and of its culture."

Cut for Purpose was created in collaboration with Rotterdam museum Boijmans van Beuningen as an installation conceived as a "spatial tool to discover its new Street Gallery". The 600 m² gallery space was filled with 2000 cardboard sheets organised in a grid structure, into which a purpose-made space was cut for various events and activities held over a period of nine weeks. These included an office space for a writer, residency space for an art collective, a workshop for product designers, a sound room, a film set and a garden, amongst others; all of which re-imagined the potential uses of a museum space and examined the spatial dynamics of differing industries.

Cut for Purpose
2006.
Courtesy Stealth.unlimited.

Richard Sweeney

Richard Sweeney is an artist specialising in Three Dimensional Design, which he studied at Manchester Metropolitan University. He uses the manipulation of seemingly banal sheet materials such as wood, paper and cardboard to create complex sculptural forms. Sweeney's incorporation of myriad disciplines within his work—including photography and formal aspects of design as well as sculpture and craft—has seen his designs realised in both smaller, design-based contexts and, more imposing public installation forms.

The artist's work *Surface*—devised for and implemented at the 2007 Cartasia Paper Festival in Lucca, Italy—is an Autocad-produced "sliceform" comprised of numerous intersecting paper maquettes, waterproofed with paper tape and a PVA based material, and raised from the ground on wooden slatting. According to Sweeney, the decision to appropriate cardboard for his design—which he feels is unfairly dismissed as merely a crude packaging material—was derived from an interest in the synchronisation between complex constructive technique and a strong structural form. The installation appears simultaneously ethereal and beautifully skeletal, but also incredibly robust in its build and presence.

Surface
Piazza Citadella, Lucca, Italy,
2007.
Cardboard waterproofed
with PVA.
400 x 200 x 200 cm.
Courtesy the artist.
Photo Richard Sweeney.

WORKac

Demonstrating how cardboard can exceed people's expectations in its uses is WORK Architecture's Public Farm 1 (PF1). Winner of the coveted MoMA/PS1 Young Architect Program for 2008, WORKac's design filled the PS1 Contemporary Art Center's courtyard as a backdrop to its Warm Up! music series for the summer of that year.

Investigating the ecological properties of cardboard, PF1 was conceived as an 'urban farm': a playful landscape of cardboard tubes, alive with vegetation, that attempted to merge the rural with the urban, whilst also highlighting the structural possibilities of the material at hand. Tens of cardboard tubes in varying heights and dimensions— some of which could have easily been mistaken for imposing concrete structures—were used to form an overarching bridge across the art centre's courtyard, that juxtaposed with the angular concrete structure of the space below.

Featuring a number of interactive elements that included a juicer column, a mobile phone charger column, a pool, and even a chicken coop, PF1 became an urban, rural sanctuary, in the middle of New York City. Not only this but WORKac stayed true to their word in regards to sustainability, with PF1 becoming a fully functioning farm, producing 50+ varieties of organic fruit, vegetables and herbs that were subsequently used by the museum's café and picked by visitors.

Urban Farm
2008.
Cardboard tubes,
vegetation and water.
Courtesy Work.

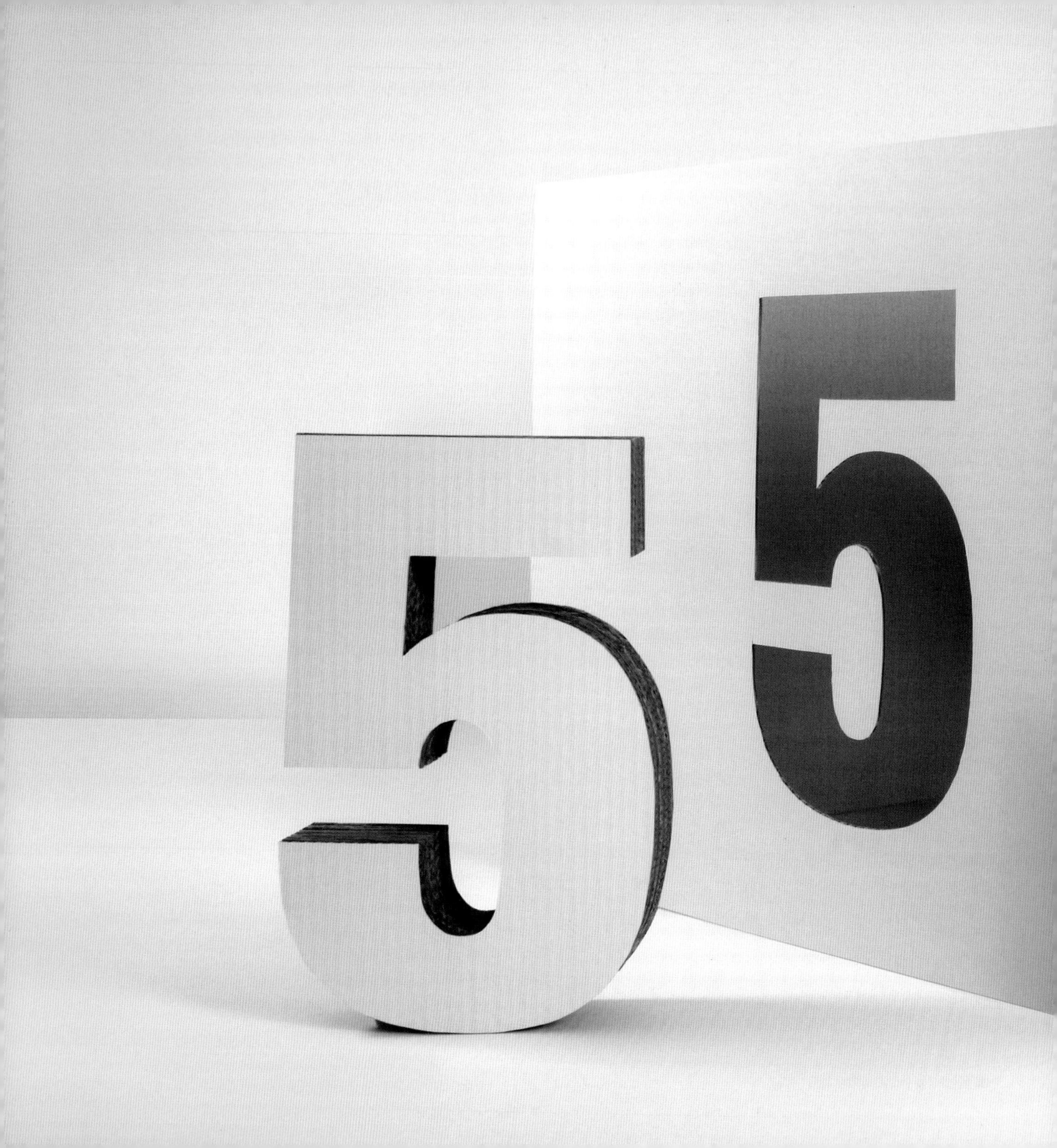

End
Matter

Acknowledgements

Thank you to all those involved in the production of *Outside the Box: Cardboard Design Now*. First, to those who offered expert words of advice in the early stages of the book's production: Karolina Johnson at the Design Council, Richard Sweeney, Ed Boaden and Lucy Winstanley. Also a special thank you to Michael Czerwinski of The Design Museum, London, and Santiago Perez for their insightful introductory essays on the many different facets of cardboard design. Many thanks must also go to each of the designers, studios and artists, and their representative galleries, featured—of whom generously donated their work to this volume.

Finally, a special thanks to those here at Black Dog Publishing—in particular to the book's designer Alex Wright for his original design and photography featured throughout, with assistance from Johanna Bonnevier and Leonardo Collina. In editorial, thank you to Tom Howells, Owain Mumford, Jon Aye, Jonno Ovans and Hannah Carnegie for their assistance throughout.

Phoebe Adler
Black Dog Publishing Limited, London UK.

Colophon

Black Dog Publishing Limited
10a Acton Street, London WC1X 9NG
United Kingdom

Tel: +44 (0)20 7713 5097
Fax: +44 (0)20 7713 8682
info@blackdogonline.com
www.blackdogonline.com

British Library Cataloguing-in-Publication Data. A CIP record for this book is available from the British Library.
ISBN 978 1 907317 10 1

Black Dog Publishing Limited, London, UK, is an environmentally responsible company. *Outside the Box: Cardboard Design Now* is printed on an FSC certified paper.

architecture art design
fashion history photography
theory and things

black dog
publishing
london uk

recycle reuse reduce

www.blackdogonline.com